About the auth

Chris Abbott is the Programme Coordinator and Researcher at Oxford Research Group, responsible for ORG's sustainable security project and editor of *sustainable*security.org. Previously he has worked as a campaigner and researcher on a number of social and environmental issues. In addition to writing several ORG reports, his articles on global security issues have appeared in various publications, both in the UK and abroad.

Paul Rogers is Professor of Peace Studies at the University of Bradford, and Global Security Consultant to Oxford Research Group. He has worked in the field of international security, arms control and political violence for over thirty years, lecturing at universities and defence colleges in several countries, and has written over twenty books. He is a regular commentator on global security issues in both the national and international media.

John Sloboda is Executive Director of Oxford Research Group. He is also Professor of Psychology and Honorary Research Fellow in the School of International Relations, Politics and the Environment at Keele University. He co-founded and manages Iraq Body Count, which quickly became a key source of information about civilian casualties during the Iraq war and its aftermath. In July 2004, John was elected to the Fellowship of the British Academy.

About Oxford Research Group

Oxford Research Group (ORG) is an independent non-governmental organisation which seeks to bring about positive change on issues of national and international security. Established in 1982, it is now considered to be one of the UK's leading global security think tanks and was voted one of the 'Top 20 Think Tanks in the UK' by the *Independent*. ORG is a registered charity and uses a combination of innovative publications, expert roundtables, residential consultations, and engagement with opinion-formers and government, to develop and promote sustainable global security strategies. **www.oxfordresearchgroup.org.uk**

About this book

This book is based on *Global Responses to Global Threats: Sustainable Security for the 21st Century*, published by Oxford Research Group in June 2006. Fully revised, updated and expanded, this current work has involved nearly two years of research in total as part of a long-term ORG project aimed at assessing the various threats to global security and developing and promoting sustainable responses to those threats. If you would like to order a bulk quantity of *Beyond Terror*, please call the Random House Sales Development Department on tel. (0)20 7840 8487.

Beyond Terror
The Truth About the Real Threats to Our World

Chris Abbott, Paul Rogers and John Sloboda

RIDER

LONDON · SYDNEY · AUCKLAND · JOHANNESBURG

1 3 5 7 9 10 8 6 4 2

First published by Oxford Research Group in 2006 as *Global Responses to Global Threats*

This updated and revised edition first published in 2007 by Rider, an imprint of Ebury Publishing, Random House, 20 Vauxhall Bridge Road, London SW1V 2SA

Random House Australia (Pty) Limited
20 Alfred Street, Milsons Point, Sydney,
New South Wales 2061, Australia

Random House New Zealand Limited
18 Poland Road, Glenfield,
Auckland 10, New Zealand

Random House South Africa (Pty) Limited
Isle of Houghton, Corner Boundary Road & Carse O'Gowrie
Houghton 2198, South Africa

Random House Publishers India Private Limited
301 World Trade Tower, Hotel Intercontinental Grand Complex
Barakhamba Lane, New Delhi 110 001, India

The Random House Group Limited Reg. No. 954009

The Random House Group Limited makes every effort to ensure that the papers used in our books are made from trees that have been legally sourced from well-managed and credibly certified forests. Our paper procurement policy can be found on www.randomhouse.co.uk

The cover of this book has been printed using vegetable inks

Original diagrams by Helen Scott
Printed and bound in Great Britain by Bookmarque Ltd, Croydon

A CIP catalogue record for this book is available from the British Library

ISBN 978–1–8460–4070–2

Contents

Acknowledgements

Oxford Research Group gratefully acknowledges the support of the Joseph Rowntree Charitable Trust, the Polden-Puckham Charitable Foundation and our many supporters and sustainers for making the publication of this book possible. The authors would like to thank Janet Bloomfield, Scilla Elworthy, James Kemp and others at ORG for their valuable help and insights, and Vanessa Shields, Emily Esplen and Wendy Conway Lamb for additional research as the work developed. They would also like to thank Judith Kendra and Sue Lascelles at Rider for being a pleasure to work with on the publication of this book.

Politics is the art of looking for trouble, finding it whether it exists or not, diagnosing it incorrectly, and applying the wrong remedy.

Sir Ernest Benn

1.

A Clear and Present Danger?

The people can always be brought to the bidding of the leaders. That is easy. All you have to do is tell them they are being attacked and denounce the pacifists for lack of patriotism and exposing the country to danger. It works the same way in any country.

Hermann Goering

Introduction

The sight of planes flying into the Twin Towers in New York on 11 September 2001 has become an iconic image of our times. That day affected people in so many different ways, but in most of the world horror, sadness, disbelief, anger and solidarity were the immediate responses to the events unfolding live on our televisions. The next day the French liberal newspaper *Le Monde* famously summed up the mood by declaring: 'Nous sommes tous Américains' – we are all Americans.[1]

During the five years that have followed those attacks, the sentiments of that headline have been squandered. The ongoing 'war on terror' and, in particular, the invasion of Iraq mean that not many people feel the same way; the concern over al-Qaida is now almost equalled by the anger felt at America and its allies. However, one thing from that day which has remained is an almost unquestioned belief that international terrorism is one of, if not *the*, greatest threats to security that we face.

For example, an unexpected outcome of the build-up to the US presidential election in 2004 was the rebirth of the long dead Committee on the Present Danger (CPD). First formed in 1950, the committee focused on convincing the American public and politicians of the grave danger posed by the Soviet Union. Following the end of the Cold War, the committee slipped back into the shadows. However, in July 2004 it re-formed to face what it considers another clear and present danger to the United States: international Islamic terrorism.

The organisation's website, which flashes up photos of

terrorist attacks in New York, Madrid and London, asserts that the organisation is dedicated to 'protecting and expanding democracy by winning the global war against terrorism and the movements and ideologies that drive it'.[2] The committee is co-chaired by former CIA director James Woolsey, who is well known to consider the fight against what the CPD calls 'global radical Islamist and fascist terrorist movements' to be World War Four (with World War Three having been the Cold War).[3]

They, and others like them, have replaced 'red under the bed' with 'terrorist at the gate' – complete with the paranoia and climate of fear associated with such a mind-set. This climate sets the context for the claim that 'terrorism is the greatest twenty-first-century threat'. This claim has become a mantra of Western leaders, and has been stamped on the public consciousness by constant press and media hype. However, is international terrorism really the single greatest threat to world security? If not, how can the 'war on terror' help us deal with the real threats we face?

Identifying Trends

Contemporary threats are often interconnected. Led, in large part, by the United Nations, there is growing international awareness that problems such as international terrorism or armed conflict cannot be dealt with in isolation from those of extreme poverty or environmental degradation.[4] These are all global issues, which threaten human security as well as state security, and they recognise no national borders.

9/11 demonstrated in the most dramatic way that rich

Western countries cannot insulate themselves from developments taking place elsewhere. It also illustrated the way that the different societies that make up humanity are interconnected and interdependent today as never before: according to the World Bank, the economic consequences of the attacks probably led to tens of thousands more children dying worldwide and millions more people living below the poverty line.[5] So only by working together will countries be able to overcome the threats they face.

To do this, though, we need to understand the nature and extent of the various threats to both our national security and wider international security. It is not enough simply to insist that terrorism is the greatest threat to the world, when the evidence does not support this claim. In fact, our research paints a very different picture of the fundamental threats that we all face, with these threats coming from four interconnected trends:

- **climate change**
- **competition over resources**
- **marginalisation of the majority world**
- **global militarisation**

There are, of course, other trends to consider, but those we have concentrated on are the ones that are most likely to lead to large-scale loss of life – of a magnitude unmatched by other potential threats – and have the greatest potential to spark violent conflict, civil unrest or destabilisation that threatens the international system as we know it. These trends are also interrelated. Progress in mitigating against one of them can be undone

Terrorism – the Greatest Threat to the World?

Many world leaders seem to agree that terrorism is the greatest danger we face:

'Terrorism is the greatest twenty-first-century threat.'

British Prime Minister Tony Blair, May 2003

'Terrorism is the greatest threat facing free democracies in the twenty-first century.'

German Chancellor Angela Merkel, May 2006

'The greatest threat this world faces is the danger of extremists and terrorists armed with weapons of mass destruction.'

US President George W. Bush, September 2005

'No challenge is greater than the threat of terrorism.'

Australian Prime Minister John Howard, May 2006

'Terrorism is the greatest threat to world peace.'

Russian President Vladimir Putin, September 2000

But are they right?

by poor decisions made in relation to another.

Another important trend, that of international terrorism, is discussed throughout the book as it will continue to dominate Western security policies, particularly those of the United States and its principal allies. While terrorism is unlikely to be a major driver of global insecurity in itself, it can be encouraged by current approaches to security and the factors outlined above. As we will show, however, current approaches are based on a flawed understanding of movements such as al-Qaida. This means that the policies currently promoted to deal with the threat of terrorism are inadequate and inappropriate.

The task today is to develop global responses to these global threats. The Cold War way of thinking focused on security as 'defence'. This approach has continued to dominate attitudes to international security, even though the global trend in major armed conflict and inter-state wars has continued to decrease in the post-Cold War era and new challenges have emerged to threaten peace and security. The failure of unilateral national solutions means we now need collective security which promotes a shared and sustainable responsibility for managing these new threats and has respect for international law and fundamental human rights at its heart.

What is needed to replace the current approach is a system of 'sustainable security' that addresses the security concerns of all peoples and tackles the root causes of both old and new threats.[6]

Our analysis may, at times, appear to be centred on the United States. This is necessary because recent US approaches to foreign policy and multilateralism have severely hampered

Beyond Terror – the Truth About the Real Threats to our World

- Terrorism is not the greatest threat to the world.
- The 'war on terror' is failing and actually increasing the likelihood of more terrorist attacks.
- Climate change is a major security concern; fortunately we have the means to address it.
- Nuclear power cannot help us combat climate change or meet our energy needs safely.
- Our quest for resources, especially oil, is causing conflict and insecurity.
- There is a direct link between foreign policy, marginalisation and political violence.
- The development and spread of WMD by our own governments puts us all at risk.
- We need a radical rethink of security policies in order to avoid a highly unstable future.
- There is still time to make a difference.

many of the efforts to address the problems covered in this book. In some instances US policies have actually added to those problems – though they are by no means alone in this. The long-term effects of this, both in the United States and elsewhere, are still unclear at present – though the serious effects on many international events are already apparent. Furthermore, the US is now the most influential global actor and the only country with a truly global military reach, and this further increases its impact on the security and political issues we are exploring.

The fundamental problem is that the global security agenda is being hijacked by the 'war on terror' and its current flashpoints in Afghanistan, Iraq and, potentially, Iran.

This, coupled with the continued pursuit of narrow national and economic interests, is distracting governments from the genuine threats that humanity faces, causing their responses to these threats to be wholly inadequate. Governments and concerned citizens worldwide must engage in constructive debate and work together to redress the balance. This book is one contribution to the debate. But it goes further than that and proposes courses of action for readers from all backgrounds to help contribute to a more secure future for us and our planet.

We hope to convince you of the real, fundamental threats to our security. We need to do this, because your commitment and action is crucial to averting these dangers. The solutions are there; they do not have to be invented. But they do have to be implemented, and that will require courage, effort, and some sacrifice, by politicians, by institutions, and by ordinary people. Governments cannot easily summon up the will to address these huge problems unless they know that they are required by the people to do so.

By the time you have finished reading this book, we hope you will have a better understanding of the issues involved, know what needs to be done, and have the knowledge and resources in your hand which will assist you in making your personal, and much needed, contribution to the solution.

2.

Climate Change

Global warming is real. We're responsible for it. The consequences are very bad and getting worse, and headed toward catastrophic unless we act quickly. But we can fix it, and we can fix it because it's not too late.

Al Gore

Climate change as a result of human activity has long been accepted as real by all but the strongest of sceptics. However, in recent years it has become obvious that climate change is not just an environmental issue but also a security concern, as it threatens the social and political stability on which all else depends.

The Pentagon's Office of Net Assessment (ONA) now identifies climate change as a threat which vastly eclipses that of terrorism. A report commissioned by the head of the ONA, Pentagon insider Andrew Marshall, and published in late-2003, concluded that climate change over the next twenty years could result in a global catastrophe costing millions of lives in wars and natural disasters. The report's authors argue that the risk of abrupt climate change should be 'elevated beyond a scientific debate to a US national security concern'.[1]

Anyone doubting the serious security implications of environmental disasters, even for rich and powerful countries such as the United States, should simply look at the large-scale loss of life and breakdown of society that occurred in New Orleans and other Gulf Coast cities (as well as rising petrol prices across the world) in a matter of days following Hurricane Katrina in August and September 2005. This is especially worrying because there has been a near doubling in the number of category 4 and 5 storms such as Katrina in the last thirty-five years, most likely as a result of rises in the temperature of the surface levels of the sea.[2]

The Social Impacts of Climate Change

In January 2004, the UK government's chief scientific adviser, Sir David King, wrote a guest editorial for the journal *Science*, warning that 'climate change is the most severe problem that we are facing today, more serious even than the threat of terrorism'. He argues that as a result of global warming 'millions more people around the world may in future be exposed to the risk of hunger, drought, flooding, and debilitating diseases such as malaria'.[3] There is further agreement from Professor John Aston, the UK foreign secretary's special representative for climate change, who believes 'we need to treat climate change not as a long-term threat to our environment but as an immediate threat to our security and prosperity'.[4]

Though there are still some sceptics, often supported by well-funded disinformation campaigns (more about this later), most scientists now agree that there has been a considerable increase in atmospheric carbon dioxide levels, mainly as a result of human activity such as burning fossil fuels and the cutting down of the world's forests, which has led to a global average temperature increase.

Representing the combined views of hundreds of the world's leading scientists, the Intergovernmental Panel on Climate Change (IPCC) predicts a future temperature rise of 1.4°C to 5.8°C by the end of the century.[5] If the eventual increase is anywhere near the higher end of this range, it would rapidly increase thermal expansion of the sea and global ice melting, resulting in an alarming rise in sea levels and a significant redrawing of the world map.[6]

Among the many consequences of this rise in sea levels

are the effects on metropolitan areas. As most of the world's large cities are positioned on coasts it could mean a large proportion of them would be lost to the sea. The gradual displacement of peoples from island, coastline and river delta areas could number in the tens of millions and the economic and social consequences would be disastrous as environmental refugees move into overpopulated inland areas already lacking sufficient resources.[7]

It is estimated that between 10 and 25 million environmental refugees have currently been displaced due to desertification in Africa, large-scale development projects and natural disasters. Respected environmentalist Professor Norman Myers has demonstrated that if there is a 30cm rise in sea level by 2050 it would likely result in a further 150 million refugees.[8] While this is at the upper end of IPCC predictions for rising sea levels, it is not entirely unrealistic and the consequences are serious enough to pay attention to.

Poorer countries will be least able to deal with this as they lack the resources and infrastructure to adapt to these, and other, social impacts of climate change. In fact, some of the early effects of global warming are already apparent. In 2004, for example, the World Health Organisation estimated that current mortality attributable to human-induced climate change was at least 150,000 people per year – with the highest proportion of these deaths occurring in Southern Africa.[9]

Estimated mortality attributable to climate change (right). (Source: World Health Organisation.)

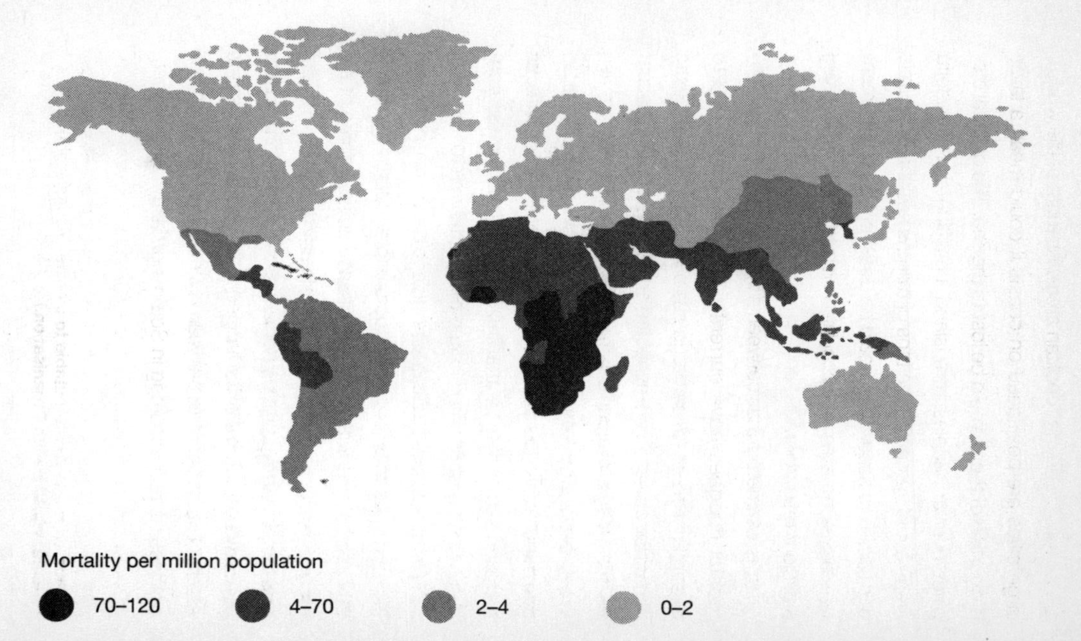
Mortality per million population
70–120
4–70
2–4
0–2

There are also persuasive arguments that climate change is likely to involve elements of 'positive feedback' in that it will encourage further environmental changes that will lead to further warming.

One possibility is that the melting of Arctic sea ice – already disappearing at a rate of 9 per cent a decade – will result in more open water during Arctic summers which will absorb more solar radiation, speeding up the process of ice melting (which could also affect the flow of the Gulf Stream).[10] Losing the sea ice of the Arctic is likely to cause dramatic changes in the climate of the northern region and will have a very big impact on other climate parameters.[11] These changes would be effectively irreversible.

A second possibility is that the progressive melting of Arctic and near-Arctic permafrost will release large volumes of methane from rotting vegetation which is, itself, an even more potent cause of climate change than carbon dioxide.

There are now substantial indications that over the next fifty years there will also be considerable shifts in the distribution of rainfall, with more rain tending to fall on the oceans and polar regions and progressively less falling on the tropical land masses. The tropics support a substantial part of the human population, much of it surviving by subsistence agriculture. A shift in rainfall distribution is likely to cause a partial drying-out of some of the most fertile regions of the tropics, resulting in a significant reduction in the ecological carrying-capacity of the land and decreases in food production.[12] China and India, in particular, could be hugely affected, with profound national and regional implications. Many of the countries in this region would have very little capacity to respond to such changes, and the resulting persistent food shortages and even famines would lead to increased suffering, greater social unrest and the pressure of greatly increased migration.

Governments should not underestimate the importance of this as it is likely to become one of the greatest of all causes of insecurity over the next half century.

While Africa will be most affected by drought and desertification due to climate change, researchers are also reporting a general drying out of the land and spread of desertification in the Mediterranean region. One of the worst droughts on record hit Spain and Portugal in 2005 and halved some crop yields, causing both countries to apply to the EU for food assistance. Droughts have also badly affected crops in Australia, and one in six countries in the world face food shortages because of severe droughts that could become semi-permanent as a result of climate change.[13] In fact, new government-funded climate prediction research by the UK Met Office indicates that extreme drought, during which agriculture becomes impossible, could affect about a third of the planet by the end of the century.[14]

The Urgency of the Problem

Greenhouse gas emissions need to be rapidly reduced in order to stabilise their atmospheric concentrations. Time is of the essence and we must make changes now.

The average temperature of the earth's surface has risen by 0.6°C since reliable records began in the late 1800s, and it is likely that the increase during the twentieth century was greater than any other century during the last thousand years.[15] The European Union believes that the eventual rise in the global average temperature must be kept to within 2°C of pre-industrial levels to ensure the continued safety of the human population.

However, some leading climate scientists suggest that if the concentration of carbon dioxide (CO_2) in the atmosphere exceeds 400 parts per million (ppm), then there will be little hope of achieving this goal. The concentration of CO_2 in the atmosphere is currently 378 ppm, and increasing by about 1.5 ppm per year.[16] If the scientists are correct, that means the 400 ppm point will be reached around 2020, and there are widespread doubts that levels can be kept to anywhere near that concentration.

While some governments are taking this threat reasonably seriously, the reaction from the United States, among others, has been less than helpful; withdrawing from the Kyoto Protocol being their best known response to what some in the Bush administration still consider the 'myth' of climate change. Even though it accounts for only 4 per cent of the world's population, America is the world's greatest polluter – producing 20 per cent of the global emissions of greenhouse gases.[17] As the world's only superpower, the United States must face up to its responsibility to take the threat of climate change seriously and take the lead in reducing emissions.

It is also important that China and India, as two of the largest developing countries not covered by the Kyoto Protocol, be brought into greater dialogue on the issue as their energy needs grow. China is of particular concern as it currently has the second highest carbon dioxide emissions, behind the United States, with a rapidly developing economy and increasingly high levels of energy use, especially from coal-fired power stations, which are the dirtiest source of electricity. In fact, in the next ten to twenty years China looks set to overtake the United States as the world's biggest producer of greenhouse gases.[18]

Informed citizens and organisations must also work to counter the well-funded disinformation campaigns that still attempt to spread falsehoods about climate change and companies that fund the work of climate sceptics and bogus grassroots groups.

One of the worst culprits is the world's largest oil company, ExxonMobil. They have been accused by Britain's national academy of science, the Royal Society, of trying to mislead the public into believing that the role of humans in causing climate change is still in doubt. The corporation has been giving huge amounts of funding to dozens of American groups whose research into climate change has been described by the Royal Society as 'misleading'.[19]

This includes the Center for the Study of Carbon Dioxide and Global Change, which has received thousands of dollars in donations from ExxonMobil, including $25,000 in 2005.[20] The Center falsely claims on its website that 'it is highly unlikely that future increases in the air's CO_2 content will produce any global warming' and therefore, unbelievably, argues that the best thing is to 'leave well enough alone and let nature and humanity take their inextricably intertwined course. All indications are that both will be well served by the ongoing rise in atmospheric CO_2.'[21] This simply is not true.

In funding a large number of organisations ExxonMobil, and others like them, are trying to create the impression that doubts about climate change are widespread.[22] Although the individuals and groups who attempt to discredit the science on global warming are increasingly marginalised, the fact that they are so well-funded, particularly in America, makes them a growing concern given the urgency with which we must now act on climate change.

Nuclear is Not the Answer

However, the response to global warming should not, as some suggest, be the increased use of nuclear power. Even some environmentalists are now promoting the idea that nuclear energy could be the environmentally sound solution to the problem of rising levels of atmospheric carbon dioxide.

Aside from the obvious environmental, economic and safety issues associated with dealing with radioactive waste, there is a very serious global security issue that many seem to ignore.

If there was a 'nuclear renaissance' this would involve the development of facilities – reactors, waste tanks and reprocessing plants – that are potential terrorist targets,[23] as well as encourage the spread of technology and materials that once on the black market could also be used in the development of nuclear weapons by 'rogue states' or terrorist networks. The peaceful atom and the military atom are what the Swedish physicist Hannes Alven, a Nobel Prize laureate, called 'Siamese twins'. Civil nuclear activity and nuclear weapons proliferation are intimately linked: one of the 'twins' cannot be promoted without the other spreading out of control.

This is where much of the current concern over Iran's nuclear programme comes from, but it is important to note that the development of nuclear power in other countries – for example, China, the United States or Japan – is just as worrying in terms of global security.[24]

There are serious dangers associated with producing plutonium in large quantities for civil use in conditions of increasing world unrest; conditions made worse by the possible social impacts of climate change already outlined. In particular, there is real concern over the potential use of plutonium in a terrorist weapon – a radiological dispersal device (so-called 'dirty bomb') or a crude nuclear weapon. This would have a devastating impact if detonated, for example, in a capital city, but also if the threat of detonation were used to blackmail a government. The problem of safe-guarding society against these hazards could become formidable. The security measures that might become necessary would seriously affect personal freedoms and have genuine consequences for democracy.[25]

It is important to appreciate that nuclear energy is *not* a carbon-free technology. Electricity is used in many stages of the nuclear cycle – from building reactors to waste disposal and decommissioning – and this electricity will mainly have been produced from fossil fuels. Even under the most favourable conditions, the nuclear cycle will produce approximately one-third as much CO_2 emission as gas-fired electricity production.

Nuclear power could only supply the entire world electricity demand for three years before sources with low uranium content would have to be mined. Given that one of the main factors is the amount of carbon dioxide produced by the mining and milling of uranium ore, the use of the poorer ores in nuclear reactors would produce more CO_2 emission than

Going it Alone – California Leads the United States on Climate Change

Republican governor Arnold Schwarzenegger has surprised and delighted environmentalists around the world by pitting California in direct opposition to Washington, and effectively signing the Kyoto Protocol on behalf of the people of California.

His tough and ambitious measures have received bipartisan support, and a broad popular mandate. They include requiring all major industries, such as car manufacturers and power companies to make drastic and progressive cuts in carbon emissions over a twenty-year period. California is one of the world's largest economies, and so California's actions have global impact.

Schwarzenegger has been effective in arguing that his measures will be good for business; and he has persuaded high-profile international business leaders such as Virgin Unite's Richard Branson, to give his programmes high-profile support. He has also gained prominent support from key national leaders, including the prime ministers of Britain and Japan.

The key mechanism in California was Assembly Bill 32, a 'first-in-the-world' wide-reaching ~

burning fossil fuels directly, and might actually consume more electricity than it produces.[26] Furthermore, the problems of the depletion of uranium mineable at economic prices would become as serious as the depletion of oil and gas if a significant nuclear renaissance were to occur.

programme of market and regulatory mechanisms, signed in September 2006 and aimed at achieving real, quantifiable, cost-effective reductions of greenhouse gases. The governor, who has accused George W. Bush of failing to show leadership on climate change, has recently sent his environmental guru Terry Tamminen out to convince other states to follow California's example. 'What California is doing can be replicated by other states,' Tamminen says. 'We can create over the next few years a *de facto* national policy on climate change and we don't have to wait for the federal government.'

Leading Republicans in states such as Arizona, Indiana and New Mexico are increasingly distancing themselves from the Bush administration. These include front-running Republican presidential candidate John McCain. They could be the key to 'cascading' similar legislation around the United States.

The momentum could be unstoppable so long as concerned American citizens (and friends of the United States around the world) continue to loudly support these initiatives, and watch like hawks to make sure they are followed through.

Therefore, while some may argue that nuclear energy could provide a 'solution' to climate change, the implications of such developments would be disastrous.

The UK government's own advisory body, the Sustainable Development Commission, concluded in March 2006 that nuclear power was dangerous, expensive and unnecessary.[27] The House of Commons Environmental Audit Committee reached similar conclusions the following month, raising serious concerns relating to safety, the threat of terrorism, and the proliferation of nuclear power across the world.[28]

So, rather than constructing new nuclear reactors, attention should be focused on the protection and security of existing facilities and options for phasing out their use altogether.

Renewable Energy

Fortunately, there is no need to rely on nuclear energy as an alternative to the current dependence on fossil fuels which is contributing so much to climate change. A more sustainable and secure response is the rapid development of local renewable energy sources – wind, wave, tidal, solar and biomass – and comprehensive energy efficiency and conservation practices. This needs to be coupled with effective carbon sequestration projects (such as planting trees) to speed up the removal of carbon dioxide from the atmosphere.

In 2003, the Institute for Sustainable Solutions and Innovations (ISUSI) found that today's technology could allow a highly developed industrialised country to completely cover its energy needs with local renewable energy sources, particularly solar and wind energy. Using the example of Japan,

ISUSI concluded that it is possible to radically reduce and eventually eliminate fossil fuels and nuclear power without reducing living standards or industrial capacity.[29]

Another more recent study by the Environmental Change Institute at the University of Oxford found that wind, solar and combined heat and power (co-generation) could together meet the electricity demand of England and Wales.[30] The UK is particularly well suited to the development of wind power, as the wind tends to blow more strongly during the day and the winter months, when energy demands from the national grid are greatest.[31]

This is one of the advantages of renewable energy sources because they tend to produce greater levels of electricity during peak demand points of the day (between 6 a.m. and midnight) and during the months of highest demand (winter months), whereas nuclear power can only produce a constant 'base-load' twenty-four hours a day, 365 days a year.[32]

Diverting resources and personnel from military science to civilian renewable energy programmes would greatly help to accelerate the technological developments already happening in this important area – for example, third generation photovoltaic concentrator cells for solar power. However, the 'war on terror' has had the effect of reversing the drop in military expenditure that followed the end of the Cold War. For example, in 2003 to 2004 the UK spent about £2.7 billion on military research and development – approximately 30 per cent of all UK government research and development spending. Overall, in 2003 the world's military spent a massive $956 billion.[33] By 2005, this had risen to $1,118 billion.[34]

A substantial proportion of this funding should be reallocated to civil uses, with an emphasis on the development of renewable energy technologies.

A rapid move towards local renewable energy sources and energy efficient practices (with low carbon and carbon neutral sources providing interim supplies) would greatly help efforts to combat climate change as well as reduce the security and political risks associated with a reliance on nuclear energy programmes and/or fossil fuel supplies from increasingly unstable regions of the world.

It is no longer a question of economics or technology: it is now purely a matter of finding the political will to make it happen.

Overview

- The effects of climate change are likely to lead to the displacement of peoples from island, coastline and river delta areas, to severe natural disasters and increasing food shortages. This would contribute to increased human suffering, greater social unrest, revised patterns of living and the pressure of higher levels of migration across the world.
- This has long-term security implications for all countries which are far more serious, lasting and destructive than those of international terrorism.
- However, the response to climate change should not be greater use of nuclear power, which would only encourage the spread of technology and materials that could be used in the development of nuclear weapons and their use by 'rogue states' or terrorist networks.
- Instead, a more secure and reliable response is the development of local renewable energy sources and radical energy conservation practices.

3.

Competition Over Resources

For everyone on earth to live at the current European average level of consumption, we would need more than double the biocapacity actually available – the equivalent of 2.1 planet Earths – to sustain us. If everyone consumed at the US rate, we would require nearly five.

The New Economics Foundation

The 'limits to growth' debate of the 1970s was prompted by an early systems analysis study of the increasing human impact on the global ecosystem. It also did much to stimulate the early development of the environmental movement. The original study of the same name, published in 1971 a few months before the UN Stockholm Environment Conference, was relatively crude and was much derided by market economists. While it was not predicting major problems for several decades, it did argue the case that there were limits to the capability of the global ecosystem to survive the effects of human activity, not least in terms of pollution, resource depletion and food shortages.[1]

In spite of the early criticisms, the experience of the past thirty years has done much to support elements of the *Limits to Growth* thesis. This includes depletion of maritime resources, erosion of biodiversity, global pollution problems such as ozone depletion, and problems of deforestation. These, together with shortages of water resources and long-term issues of human malnutrition and famine are likely to remain major factors in the coming decades, but there are also issues of resource depletion and potential conflict that are becoming particularly pertinent.

Of greatest significance are the problems now being caused by an excessive reliance on fossil fuels, especially oil and natural gas. Both as a source of conflict and as a major factor in climate change, the location and exploitation of oil, in particular, is of massive if largely unrecognised importance.

The Resource Shift

Current problems need to be put in historical context. An important aspect of industrialisation in Western Europe and North America was that the initial period of industrial growth in the nineteenth century could be based on domestic resources. Britain, for example, had indigenous supplies of coal, iron ore, copper, lead and tin that were more than adequate throughout most of the century.

By the mid-twentieth century this had changed dramatically and most Western European states had become heavily dependent on imported raw materials, so much so that states in the Global South became locked into the world economy as suppliers of low cost primary products.[2] In the last fifty years, even the United States has become a net importer of many primary products.

This long-term international trend has been termed the 'resource shift' and is a key factor in international political economy. On occasions it leads to intense competition and even conflict – recent examples have included open conflict over cobalt in Zaire in the late 1970s, more recent conflict in the Great Lakes over tantalum supplies (used in mobile phones), and protracted conflict over diamonds in West Africa.

While these are significant in the regions concerned, they are not a focus of global conflict, but this is not the case for oil. It is here that the resource shift is at its most remarkable, and it is a combination of increasing dependence of major industrial states on imported oil, with the very limited location of key oil reserves, that is significant.

Although Norway is still self-sufficient in oil through its North Sea reserves, the United Kingdom is no longer in this position because of the depletion of major fields, and the UK is now therefore joining the rest of Western Europe as a net oil importer. In any case, the North Sea fields are small compared with global reserves – even at their peak in the early 1990s, they made up barely 3 per cent of the world total (compared with over 65 per cent for the Persian Gulf region).

Another major industrial power, Japan, has long been a major oil importer, as has South Korea, but it is the position of the United States and China that is key. Until around 1970, the United States was able to use its major oil fields in Texas, California, Louisiana and the Gulf of Mexico to provide for just about all its needs. From the start of the 1970s, the domestic oil fields were no longer able to keep up with demand, and even the development of the North Slope and Prudhoe Bay fields in Alaska made little difference as demand soared. Over the following thirty years the United States saw production fall as demand rose, and the end result was a massive dependence on imported oil by the end of the century.[3]

Oil and US Security

Even in the 1970s, oil security began to figure prominently in US military thinking, and the massive oil price hike of 1973–4 (over 400 per cent rise in nine months) had a radical effect on the US defence posture. This was primarily because the Persian Gulf was becoming the world's main region for oil production, exports and reserves, and there were severe doubts as to whether the US had the military capability to intervene in the region should the Soviet Union or a regional state take action to interrupt supplies.

As a result of these fears, the Joint Rapid Deployment Task Force was established by the Pentagon at the end of the 1970s and was later elevated into an entirely new unified military command, US Central Command (CENTCOM) in the mid-1980s. CENTCOM's zone of responsibility was centred on the Persian Gulf, extending to South West Asia and North East Africa, and it was CENTCOM under General Norman Schwarzkopf that was the centre of the coalition of forces that evicted the Iraqis from Kuwait in 1991.[4]

After the 1991 War, CENTCOM remained a major focus for the US military posture which included the re-establishment of the US Navy's Fifth Fleet to cover the Persian Gulf and the Indian Ocean. It also maintained large military bases in Saudi Arabia in spite of bitter opposition from Islamic radicals who saw the presence of a foreign power in the Kingdom of the Two Holy Places (Mecca and Medina) as entirely unacceptable. This became sufficient to deter the United States from expanding its operations in Saudi Arabia, but other states such as Kuwait and Qatar were readily available, as was the key logistics base of Diego Garcia in the Indian Ocean.

While CENTCOM, with its hundreds of planes, scores of warships and several hundred thousand troops, had an immediate focus on the autocratic regime of Saddam Hussein and the radical Islamic Republic of Iran, there is also a longer-term concern over trends in oil supplies and markets, in which China is rapidly becoming significant. This is partly because China, like the United States, can no longer produce enough oil from domestic fields and increasingly needs to import oil from the Gulf, and partly because of the overwhelming importance of the Gulf reserves.

Significantly, CENTCOM's area of responsibility has now been extended to include the Caspian Basin which, although not having oil reserves that are remotely on the scale of the Persian Gulf, is also a region in which the competing energy interests of China and the United States are becoming increasingly important (the Niger Delta is also similar in that regard, although outside of CENTCOM's area of responsibility).

The relationship between the United States and China over the issue of oil security is far more important than is commonly appreciated, not least because of China's rapidly increasing oil imports. It has taken the United States around forty years to get from the point where it was self-sufficient in oil supplies to needing to import more than 50 per cent of its oil. It is taking China about half that time and it will reach that point by 2010. This is the primary reason why China has made some substantial long-term economic agreements with Iran over oil imports, and it is a principal motive behind the Pentagon's desire to 'secure' the Persian Gulf.

The Persian Gulf

As of 2005, world oil reserves stand at approximately 1 trillion barrels. Of this, around 260 billion barrels are located in Saudi Arabia, with these being by far the largest reserves in any one country.[5] Even so, the second, third, fourth and fifth countries are also in the Persian Gulf region – Iraq, Iran, Kuwait and the

Woking and Dongtan – Beacons for Energy Self-Sufficiency

Woking, a quite unremarkable town in a politically conservative region of Britain has achieved a small miracle. Its town centre has become completely energy self-sufficient. It even produces a small surplus to sell. It has done this by creating its own electricity grid, quite independent of the national grid, connected up to numerous 'mini' power stations, generating electricity by a variety of renewable means.

In the daytime, thousands of rooftop photovoltaic cells convert sunlight into power. At night, power is supplied by a power station using fuel-cell technology, a renewable source that uses waste hydrogen from other industrial processes. Not only does Woking's fuel-cell generator provide power, it also produces a million litres per year of clean water as a by-product.

Woking shows how creativity can transform existing urban systems. China is showing the world how to build a new eco-friendly city from scratch. Dongtan, a city designed to house 800,000 people, is being constructed on Chiongming Island, near Shanghai. The vision is to build a community with low energy consumption that will be carbon-free.

It will make full use of the latest in alternative energies, petrol and diesel vehicles will be banned and there will be special devices to capture rain and store it for residents. In addition, all the energy needed for the city will be generated by Dongtan itself. ~

> Buildings will have photovoltaic solar panels, and there will be large wind turbines outside the city area with smaller ones on buildings. Biomass energy production, using waste products, will also be used. This will make use of organic waste – such as the millions of rice husks (the outer shell of a rice plant) thrown away each day – to produce power. Buildings will also be for mixed use, combining work and residential areas to minimise commuting.
>
> Projects like Woking and Dongtan show what is possible everywhere. Local politicians will start to act if their residents get together and demand it. Many towns and cities now have citizen-led sustainability groups: lend them your voice.

United Arab Emirates. These together have close to two-thirds of *all* the proven reserves in the world (see figure overleaf for a comparison with other regions). Moreover, the oil tends to be of high quality, much of it is cheap to extract from land-based fields, and some does not even need to be pumped up from underground but comes to the surface under pressure.[6]

Because of the international resource shift, combined with patterns of consumption, the Persian Gulf will be the dominant location for world oil supplies for the next several decades, with the major industrial powers becoming steadily more dependent on Gulf oil.

For the United States, it is a core security requirement that it is able to deploy military forces which can maintain control

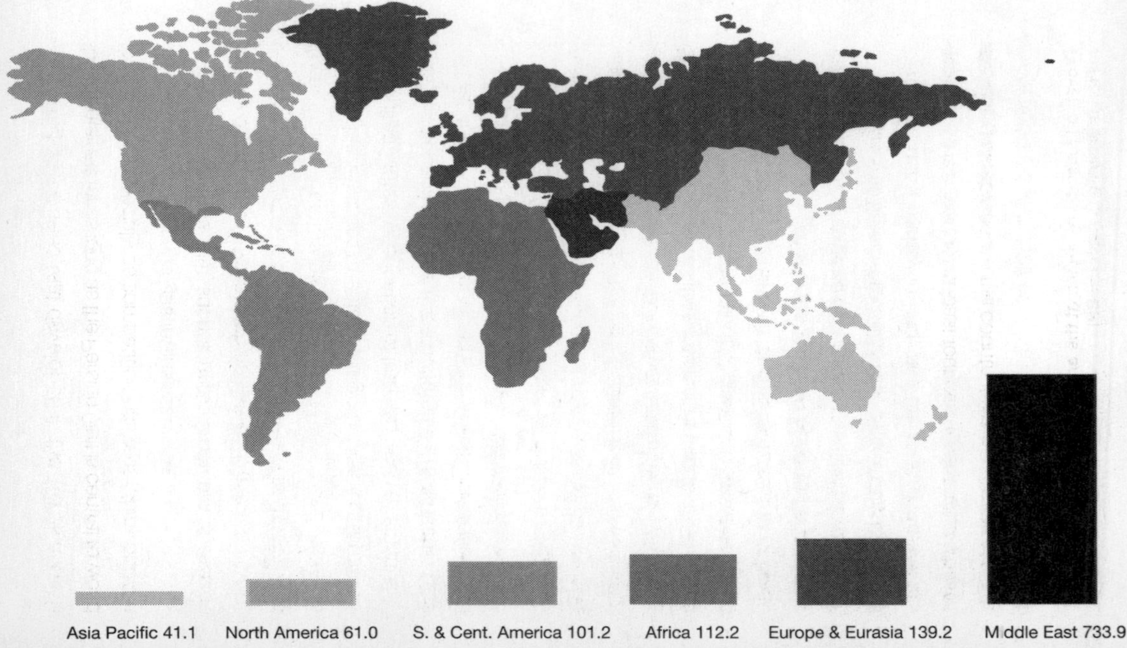
Asia Pacific 41.1
North America 61.0
S. & Cent. America 101.2
Africa 112.2
Europe & Eurasia 139.2
Middle East 733.9

of the region – a trend that developed in the 1970s and will be maintained for as long as the Persian Gulf is central to world oil supplies, especially as competition between China and the United States for oil and gas intensifies.

The problem is that such a military posture is already bitterly opposed by states such as Iran and, even more significantly, by radical Islamic paramilitaries such as those linked to al-Qaida. For the al-Qaida movement itself, with its improbable vision of re-establishing an Islamic caliphate,[7] the United States' occupation of Iraq has been a remarkably positive development for three quite different reasons. One is that the widespread coverage of civilian casualties and 'collateral damage' on satellite TV news channels such as al-Jazeera and al-Arabiya has been a powerful recruiting tool; a second is that Iraq is starting to provide a combat training zone in urban guerrilla warfare for paramilitary radicals from outside Iraq who will be able, in due course, to take their experience and capabilities into other areas of al-Qaida operations. The third reason is that Baghdad was the historic centre of the most sustained Islamic Caliphate, the Abbasid Caliphate (750 to 1250 in the Western calendar) and is now easily represented as being occupied by neo-Christian forces.[8]

At the same time, while the United States may be deeply mired in an insurgency in Iraq, any talk of a complete US withdrawal is specious. At least four permanent military bases are being established in the country (two of them near major

Proven oil reserves by region at the end of 2004 – in thousand million barrels (left). (Source: BP)

oil fields, a third near suspected substantial oil deposits and the fourth close to Baghdad), even though such a presence will be a continual source of opposition and conflict. Meanwhile, elements within the Bush administration are advocating pre-emptive military action against Iran, viewing it as another component of the 'axis of evil', and one with presumed nuclear weapons ambitions.

In a real sense, oil security and climate change are aspects of the same problem. Because of the concentration of oil reserves in the Middle East, and increasingly intense competition between the United States and China, that region stands to experience deep instability and conflict, a situation that would be greatly eased if dependence on oil could be substantially diminished. That is also an essential requirement to combat climate change, making the ending of our addiction to oil one of the most urgent issues facing the world.

Water Politics

Competition over oil is not the only resource-related issue that may lead to instability. Concerns over the availability of adequate water supplies are almost as urgent in some parts of the world. It is likely that water scarcity will exacerbate existing tensions and water supply may be used as a 'tool' within inter-state conflict that has begun for other reasons.[9] Such trends will be made worse by the impacts of climate change which look likely to substantially reduce available water in many areas of the world where water is scarce.[10]

'Water politics' already plays a part in conflict in some regions of the world, particularly the Middle East (where Israel, for example, has already taken action against Syria and Lebanon over supplies from the River Jordan). Demand for fresh water is well beyond that which can be sustained at current, much less future, levels.[11] Population growth will mean greater and greater demands on water resources, and where a number of states rely on the same water, tensions are likely to increase.

For example, the Nile river complex flows through ten countries, where half the population lives below the poverty line. The population in the Nile basin is expected to double in the next twenty-five years, creating further tensions. Egypt and Sudan have extensive rights over the river's waters and have been reluctant to renegotiate treaties on its management with other river states.[12]

A further example of such tensions is between Israel and Palestine, where both populations rely on access to many of the same water sources, especially from the winter rains that fall over the hills of the West Bank.

Water is a source of security and prosperity, and with water shortages likely to increase, with the potential to severely affect food production in some areas, some of these tensions could develop into full-scale armed conflict unless there is a strict observance of water laws and a multi-lateral approach to developing water management agreements.

Overview

- Industrialised and industrialising states are increasingly dependent on imported resources, especially oil and gas.
- Oil is currently the main marketed fossil fuel and the Persian Gulf is the dominant region, with two-thirds of world reserves. It is a deeply unstable region with continuing potential for conflict as the United States seeks to maintain control against opposition from regional state and sub-state paramilitary groups.
- There is also a longer-term concern over trends in oil supplies and markets, in which China is rapidly becoming significant. This is partly because China, like the United States, can no longer produce enough oil from domestic fields and increasingly needs to import oil from the Persian Gulf.
- Oil consumption is a primary cause of climate change and should be rapidly reduced for this reason alone. In a very real sense, the short-term nature of conflict in the Persian Gulf means that this liability of the oil-based economy should also be used to seek a rapid move to renewables.

4.

Marginalisation of the Majority World

Poverty is the worst form of violence.

Mahatma Gandhi

Despite the clear evidence of the security risks posed by climate change and related environmental issues, the US government, in particular, remains focused on projecting its influence and securing access to resources. This is increasingly undertaken through the 'war on terror', which relies on an exaggerated perceived risk of the threat of international terrorism, without addressing the underlying causes of that terrorism.

However, the US State Department's own figures show that the number of US citizens killed each year by international terrorism is rarely more than a couple of dozen.[1] Even in 2001, which saw the highest death toll from international terrorism on record, the number of Americans killed was around 2,500.[2] Now, that number of innocent people killed is horrific, but in the same year in the United States 3,500 people died from malnutrition, 14,000 people died from HIV/AIDS, and 62,000 people died from pneumonia.

The biggest killer in the United States that year was heart disease, which killed over 700,000 people. Over 30,000 Americans committed suicide and over 42,000 were killed in traffic accidents. In addition, there were nearly 30,000 firearm-related deaths and over 20,000 homicides.[3]

Of course 'number of deaths' is a somewhat crude measure of threat, which does not take into account non-fatal casualties. Also, people tend to be more alarmed by large-scale dramatic deaths than ones that constantly accumulate over time. But that does not hide the fact that in 2001 (the year of the 9/11 attacks) a US citizen was over five times more likely to die from HIV/AIDS than from international terrorism.

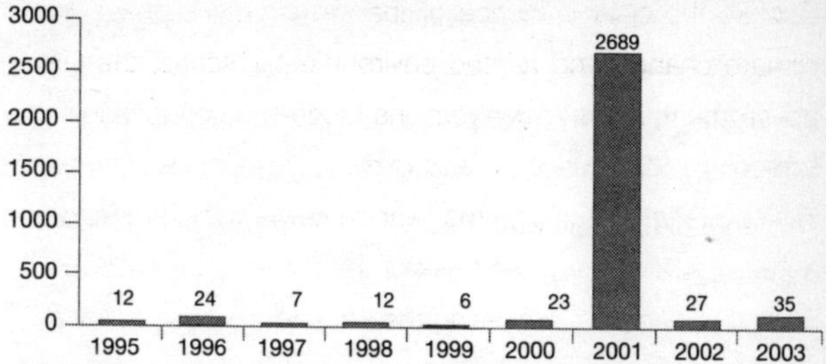

Number of US citizens killed in acts of international terrorism (1995–2003). (Source: US State Department.)

Four years on, in 2005, the United States spent only around $2.6 billion fighting HIV/AIDS globally[4] but a massive $48.5 billion on homeland security alone.[5]

The Security Implications of HIV/AIDS

Worldwide, HIV/AIDS has become the leading cause of death among adults aged fifteen to fifty-nine years old (followed by heart disease and tuberculosis). Globally, more than 20 million people have died from HIV/AIDS and 34 to 46 million others are now infected with the virus.[6] Tackling this is the world's most urgent public health challenge and UNICEF considers AIDS to be the worst catastrophe ever to hit the world,[7] yet worldwide only around $6 billion was set aside in 2004 for combating the virus.[8]

According to the UN, 70 per cent of the millions of people infected with HIV/AIDS live in Africa (25 million of these in sub-Saharan Africa), and 7.7 per cent of all Africans of working age are HIV infected. The economic destruction and massive expected deaths, with the loss of the working and parental generation, has the potential to overwhelm the social structure and medical facilities of many African countries, threatening the collapse of poor states that have been most highly infected.

This is exacerbated by two further factors. Firstly, there are currently over 12 million children orphaned by AIDS in sub-Saharan Africa – and UNICEF estimates that 18 million children in the region will have lost at least one parent to AIDS by 2010.[9] With the great societal upheaval that seems almost certain in many African countries, there is the risk that some of these children will become vulnerable to recruitment by rebels, terrorists or criminal gangs (particularly as they rarely receive the public support or services that they need).

Secondly, the armed forces in Africa tend to have a higher prevalence of the virus than the rest of the population: in some African countries as many as 50 per cent of new military recruits are HIV positive – in Zambia it is as high as 60 per cent.[10] This has a serious impact on military readiness and some countries have hesitated to participate in peacekeeping missions for fear that soldiers deployed abroad may further spread the virus or bring it back to their local communities when demobilised.[11]

This all makes HIV/AIDS more than just a humanitarian concern, but also a military and security issue – with the potential, though by no means certainty, to cause destabilisation, civil conflict or even the collapse of states.

This has been recognised by the United Nations in Security

Council Resolution 1308 (2000), which states that 'the HIV/AIDS pandemic, if left unchecked, may pose a risk to stability and security'.[12] What is clear is that HIV is one among many factors, including poverty, hunger, environmental degradation, and religious tensions, that can lead to destabilisation and conflict.[13]

Given that the vast majority of HIV infections occur in the developing world it is in many ways symptomatic of the massive socio-economic divisions that are present worldwide.

Socio-Economic Divisions

Globally, more than 1 billion people must try to survive on less than $1 a day[14] and almost half of the world's 2.2 billion children live in poverty.[15] Across the world, some 115 million children who should be in school are not – three-fifths of them girls and over a third in war-torn countries.[16] Indigenous peoples face persecution and the destruction of their lands for profit. Almost 2 billion people live in countries where regimes do not fully accommodate civil and political freedoms. About 900 million people worldwide belong to ethnic, religious or linguistic groups that face discrimination.[17]

As a result of natural disasters, war and poverty, 815 million people in developing countries are suffering from acute hunger and each year 10 million people die of hunger and hunger-related diseases, despite the fact that there is enough food available to feed the entire global population of 6.4 billion people.[18] As discussed earlier, this is something that will only get worse as a result of climate change if the flooding of river-delta and coastline areas leads to the large-scale displacement of people, and the drying out of the tropics leads to the food shortages and famine that could be expected.

There is a clear and present danger in the world today. A complex interplay of discrimination, global poverty, Third World debt, infectious disease, global inequality and deepening socio-economic divisions, together make for key elements of current global insecurity.

While overall global wealth has increased, the benefits of this economic growth have not been equally shared. The rich–poor divide is actually growing, with a very heavy concentration of growth in relatively few parts of the world, and poverty getting much worse in many other regions.

The 'majority world' of Asia, Africa and Latin America is being marginalised as North America and Europe try to maintain their political, cultural, economic and military global dominance.

Unfair international trade rules, such as the high tariffs imposed by the EU, the United States and other Western countries on imported food, clothing and other goods, prevent poorer countries from developing their economies. Aid is often in the form of loans and is tied to products coming from the donor countries, or is directly tied to the privatisation of public services. Many of the least developed nations are crippled by the huge burden of debt that has been forced on them by economic circumstance and by other governments and international financial institutions, and even debt relief often comes with strict conditions. Multinational corporations exploit the natural resources of many countries with little or no benefit to the local population and little concern for the social and environmental impacts of their actions.

This situation is often supported by the political elites in those countries, as they are usually the ones that prosper most under such circumstances, further adding to the sense of injustice within the population and often resulting in harsh repression and brutal security measures being employed by those elites. All too often, international arms companies, with the assistance of their governments, are ready and willing to provide a wide range of weapons systems, often directed at the harsh control of dissident movements, with small arms killing tens of thousands of civilians each year.[19]

Organised crime, social disorder and cultural tensions thrive in this poverty and inequality, particularly in the ever-expanding urban areas. Although there are many complex factors at play, addressing these issues would help alleviate some of the root causes of anti-elite action, political violence and international terrorism, much more than any 'war on terror' ever could.

It is, of course, a massive oversimplification to say that poverty leads to terrorism. The political aims of radical paramilitary groups, whatever their philosophies, can only be achieved if they have, among other things, the support of those whom they claim to represent and are able to muster the resources that they need. That support will depend on how deep and enduring are the grievances of those people, and the ability of the groups to tap into this underlying reservoir of discontent and marginalisation.

The success of groups such as Hezbollah in Lebanon and Hamas in the Palestinian territories, is in part due to the fact that they are able to provide the medical, educational and social

Third World Debt – Getting the Attention of Politicians

Many of the world's poorest countries are forced to pay millions of dollars every day in debt repayments, while poverty kills millions of their people. However, debt campaigning over the years has made a huge impact. In the early 1990s, before the international Jubilee movement gained momentum, politicians routinely resisted demands for debt cancellation. The Jubilee 2000 movement was born in 1990 when a tiny group of concerned students and staff at Keele University in the UK decided to act on an idea thrown up in a pub conversation. Ten years later 24 million people signed the global Jubilee 2000 petition asking the leaders of the richest countries to cancel the unpayable debts of the world's poorest countries. This, the largest petition ever, made politicians finally take notice. It all began with the creative commitment of a handful of ordinary people, with ~

services that the local governments have failed to deliver, thus securing the allegiance of a disaffected population and legitimising their violent agenda.

It is a sad fact that if talented and educated people are faced with oppression, political disenfranchisement and lack of opportunity (whether real or perceived) it creates a sense of marginalisation that may make some more likely to turn to radical and violent movements under certain circumstances – as witnessed in Saudi Arabia, Palestine, Iraq and elsewhere.

no special power or influence.

Grass roots organisations and a wide coalition of aid agencies began to mobilise their increasingly informed and motivated supporters, which meant that the issue remained on the international agenda. By 2005, there was a huge focus on the injustices of debt. Pressure on politicians resulted in agreements that should mean some of the world's poorest countries have more of their own money to spend on education, health and infrastructure.

However, much more needs to be done. Crucially, governments must end the crippling conditions attached to so much debt relief and widen the range of countries it is offered to. This work continues with the Jubilee Debt Campaign, the Make Poverty History movement and numerous religious and other organisations, all of which would benefit from your support.

In the Middle East, unemployed and disaffected youths are often referred to as the 'hayateen', the 'men who lean against walls'. It is these 'men who lean against walls' who live in political and economic conditions that make them susceptible to radical Islamist ideas. As the perceived drivers of globalisation and the prime beneficiaries of the status quo, the United States and its allies can become primary targets, alongside local elites, of this frustration.

The combination of current economic and demographic

trends with continued improvements in education and modern communications technologies, such as satellite television and the Internet, indicates that this perception of marginalisation is likely to increase rather than decrease.

The 'War on Terror'

This global trend remains unrecognised by most of the world's political elite. The 'war on terror' is distracting them from the fundamental causes of insecurity, and the need to address global poverty, political exclusion and injustice has not made it on to the national security agenda of most countries.

Instead, the current US government and its allies have chosen a geopolitical 'war on terror' as it pursues its New American Century.

Since 9/11 this has cost the US government an estimated $357 billion in military operations, reconstruction, embassy costs and various aid programmes in Iraq and Afghanistan, and for enhanced security at military bases around the world.[20]

However, the human cost has been infinitely higher.

In Iraq, now on the brink of civil war, at least 50,000 civilians[21] and thousands of Iraqi military and police have been killed as a result of the invasion. To date the US has suffered nearly 3,000 military fatalities in Iraq, with over 20,000 troops wounded in action[22] and a similar number evacuated because of non-combat injuries and severe physical or mental health problems.[23] The other members of the Coalition have lost around 250 soldiers in total, with at least half of those coming from the UK.[24]

In Afghanistan, while the Taliban may have been ousted

from power, more innocent civilians were killed as a direct result of military action there than died in the 9/11 attacks that prompted the US-led invasion,[25] and the Taliban are now a re-emerging force in many areas of the country as the conflict turns into a violent counter-insurgency operation.

In the two conflicts, the number of civilians seriously injured is likely to be in the region of 100,000, and tens of thousands have been internally displaced.

The alleged, but now generally discounted, pre-war link between Saddam Hussein's Iraq and al-Qaida has become a self-fulfilling prophecy, in that treating Iraq as part of the 'war on terror' has only spawned new terror in the region and created a combat training zone for paramilitaries and jihadists. The elusive weapons of mass destruction are rarely, if ever, mentioned any more. People across the world now overwhelmingly believe that the Iraq war has made the world a more dangerous place, and in most countries support for the 'war on terror' has declined.[26] If extended to Iran, the implications of intervention would be disastrous.[27]

The planners in Washington and London hoped that the removal of Saddam Hussein and the spreading of democracy to Iraq would eventually vindicate their policy of pre-emption. However, it has become clear that 'democracy' in this instance actually means the privatisation of state-run industries, plus elections.[28]

The US policy of detention without trial of 'unlawful combatants' in Guantánamo Bay; the widespread and deliberate bombing of civilian infrastructure in Afghanistan and Iraq; the abuse and torture of prisoners at the Abu Ghraib prison;

and the destruction of Fallujah, the 'city of mosques', are just four more of the injustices of the 'war on terror' – injustices widely reported across the Muslim world, further adding to the sense of oppression and marginalisation (Islamic militants often also cite Chechnya, Kashmir and Palestine as further examples of Western oppression of Muslims).

The US and its allies are facing a decline in their perceived legitimacy because they are not abiding by the same rules they seek to impose on others,[29] but instead, according to Amnesty International, seem to be acting on the principle that the only way to protect their security is by eroding others' human rights.[30]

This is not the way to curb recruitment to terrorist organisations or address anti-Western attitudes – as recent attacks in Islamabad, Karachi, Djakarta, Bali, Mombasa, Riyadh, Casablanca, Istanbul, Sinai, Amman, Madrid and London reveal. Moreover, as the July 2005 attacks in London may have demonstrated, these actions risk increasing support for al-Qaida and their associates among Islamic communities in Western countries, thus creating a truly transnational phenomenon of self-radicalising groups that are almost impossible to police (the focus by some governments on 'failed states' as a breeding ground for terrorists is misleading in this regard).

This is made even more likely by the harsh anti-terrorism and immigration laws enacted by some countries, which are creating a legacy of alienation and disillusionment in many Muslim communities, particularly among young people.

As the Defense Science Board (an advisory committee to

the US Secretary of Defense) concluded in September 2004, 'Muslims do not "hate our freedom", but rather they hate our policies.'[31] A post-7/7 UK Home Office working group also concluded that British foreign policy, especially in the Middle East, was 'a key contributory factor' in the motivations of radical extremists.[32]

Those denying that there is some link between the policies and abuses of the 'war on terror' – especially foreign occupation of Muslim lands – and an increase in the threat from Islamist terrorism now sound increasingly out of touch with reality. This is particularly true in Britain, where following the London tube bombings the British government remains in complete denial about any connection between its foreign policy and the suicide attacks, in many ways instead blaming the Muslim community for not doing enough to fight extremism. This is despite the fact that, while we must all work to combat extremism, polls clearly show that a huge majority of the British public believe the prime minister's foreign policy, particularly in the Middle East, has made Britain more of a target for terrorists.[33]

Given that the aim of terrorism is to terrorise and to destabilise countries by keeping them in a constant state of fear, it is somewhat sickly ironic that the 'war on terror' itself is creating a climate of fear that can be politically advantageous for those in power; a climate in which, for example, a sizeable percentage of Americans consistently, and unrealistically, report they are worried that they or someone in their family will become a victim of terrorism[34] and a majority believe there will be another terrorist attack in the United States.[35]

If 'weapons of mass destruction' or 'rogue states' are added into the mix, then that fear really begins to take hold (helped along to a great extent by the media), allowing governments to pursue policies that would otherwise be impossible.

However, while many countries are at risk of further terrorist attacks, the consequences are on a different scale to the threats we have been discussing, and much of the currently perceived threat from international terrorism is somewhat of a fear of a phantom enemy. That 'phantom enemy' is not international terrorism per se but rather a popular image of Islamic fundamentalism epitomised by what most think of as 'al-Qaida'.

Understanding Terrorism and Political Violence

It is important to appreciate that al-Qaida is not an organisation as such: it is more an ideology about freeing Muslim lands and cleansing a corrupt world through religious violence.[36] Furthermore, far from sleeper cells in every country, it is more realistic to think of al-Qaida as a 'consortium', a kind of network of networks, sharing a radical worldview but with individual 'member' groups and associates working independently of top-down leadership from Osama bin Laden and his number two Ayman al-Zawahiri, and often fighting for different local objectives (though sometimes sharing resources and support).

The broad political aims of the movement can, however, be identified as: the expulsion of foreign troops from the Middle East; termination of the House of Saud and other elitist and pro-Western regimes across the region; the elimination of Israel and the creation of a Palestinian state; and support for insurgents in other regions of the Muslim world.[37] These aims are measured in terms of decades, not years, and so today's successes and failures are very much seen as only the opening stages of a long-term battle. In one way this is a view shared to a remarkable extent by the Pentagon with its rebranding of the 'war on terror' into the 'long war'.

'Al-Qaida', if it ever really existed as most people understand it, did not survive past the end of 2001 – though some form of training centre and support base has now been re-established in northern Pakistan and southern Afghanistan. The individuals and groups so often called al-Qaida today may actually have very few substantial links to bin Laden; they merely follow similar precepts and methods – acting autonomously, but in the 'style' of al-Qaida that bin Laden now personifies.

After 9/11 and the US invasion of Afghanistan that followed, bin Laden's role in the radical Islamic movement has been limited to that of a propagandist making effective use of modern communications technology. Although opinion surveys show that confidence in bin Laden has fallen in most Muslim countries in recent years,[38] he is still considered a 'counter-cultural symbol' with cult status, representing a discourse of dissent in much of the Muslim world.[39]

Increasingly, the Internet is being used to communicate this dissent and is proving to be a powerful, anonymous and dangerous propaganda and radicalisation tool for violent Islamist groups, increasing the likelihood of surprise attacks by previously unknown 'self-generating' cells.[40]

Terrorist organisations and 'rogue states' are not isolated phenomena that can be defeated militarily on a case-by-case basis, thereby regaining control and maintaining the existing world order. Al-Qaida and the like are more of an indicator, a 'symptom', of a longer-term trend. It follows that policies to control such developments will need to go beyond the traditional, if often effective, methods of counter-terrorism to

Dialogue with Terrorists – Learning from Northern Ireland

Replacing armed confrontation with dialogue is not an idealistic fiction. It is exactly what happened between the British government and the Irish Republican Army (IRA), leading in July 2005 to the historic announcement that the IRA was ending its thirty-year 'armed campaign'.

One important aspect of ending the violence was the recognition of the root causes of that violence. The Catholic minority in Northern Ireland had suffered real marginalisation and discrimination at the hands of the Protestant majority. As the economic, social and political position of Irish Catholics was improved, so support for paramilitary violence ebbed away.

At the same time, real opportunities were created for those who supported political violence to achieve their ends through non-violent means, with participation in the democratic political process. The groundwork was achieved through extended informal contacts and discussion, away from the ~

incorporate a wide range of conflict prevention and conflict resolution methods, but going on from these to include determined efforts to address the underlying socio-economic divisions that are leading to the deep global divisions that the world is currently experiencing.

Violent groups often grow out of local conditions to address grievances, whether local or global, which they feel

public gaze, where understanding and trust was gradually achieved.

British military forces were not completely withdrawn from Northern Ireland, but their roles became increasingly preventive rather than provocative, working in collaboration with police, intelligence services and local community leaders. Three battalions of the Royal Irish Regiment are now being disbanded in 2007 when the Army formally ends Operation Banner, its official support of the police in Northern Ireland, after thirty-six years.

American military leaders such as General John Abizaid (one-time commander of US forces in Iraq) have asserted that a purely military defeat of insurgencies is not possible. It is often politicians that are failing to provide the leadership that would transform violent conflict to productive dialogue. Soldiers cannot win 'hearts and minds' when the political will of their masters is lacking. Ask your representative why the lessons of Northern Ireland are not being applied in current conflicts.

cannot be dealt with through the political system available to them. Principal among these grievances is the occupation of territory the terrorists view as their homeland and, as such, terrorist campaigns are primarily nationalistic, not religious or even particular to Islam (for example, the Hindu/secular Tamil Tigers in Sri Lanka are responsible for more suicide attacks than any other group worldwide).[41] Though of course their actions may be 'cloaked' in religion.

These groups offer radical philosophies – be they nationalistic, political or religious – that may offer people an explanation of what is happening around them, and suggest violent actions that make sense from within an environment of marginalisation, despair and anger.

Terrorism is a tactic, a means to an end. You cannot declare war on a tactic. Instead, we must give these groups (whether religious or secular, old or new) legitimate outlets for political, social and religious grievances and bring them into the political process wherever possible, no matter how painful that route may be at times. By genuinely addressing the root causes of political violence and bringing groups into dialogue, violence can be stopped.[42] In other words, the 'war on terror' should be viewed less as a 'war', than a sustained campaign to win hearts and minds.[43]

This is not to excuse terrorism in any form. To try to understand is not to condone. It is only by truly understanding terrorism and the causes of terrorism that there will be any hope of avoiding future attacks. After all, the most dangerous feature of terrorism is not necessarily the violent acts themselves, but our responses to those acts.

Overview

- While overall global wealth has increased, the benefits of this economic growth have not been equally shared, with a very heavy concentration of growth in relatively few parts of the world.
- These divisions are being exacerbated by increasing oppression and political exclusion, coupled with a growing sense of marginalisation as a result of improvements in education and modern communication technologies, leading in places to increased levels of political violence.
- Current security policies and the 'war on terror' are not reacting appropriately to this key trend, and are actually causing an increase in support for radical and violent movements such as the al-Qaida network.
- Policies to control such developments will need to go beyond traditional methods of counter-terrorism to incorporate a wide range of conflict prevention and resolution methods, but going on from these to include determined efforts to address the underlying global socio-economic divisions that the world is currently experiencing.

5.

Global Militarisation

If the world should blow itself up, the last audible voice would be that of an expert saying it can't be done.

Peter Ustinov

Outside of the two world wars, the most sustained period of militarisation was during the Cold War from the late 1940s through to the end of the 1980s. During this period, close to 85 per cent of all world military spending was undertaken by the NATO and Warsaw Pact alliances, peaking in the mid-1980s at $1 trillion per year at today's prices.[1]

As well as massive spending on conventional weapons, the two superpowers engaged in a sustained nuclear arms race that reached a peak of close to 70,000 warheads worldwide. The largest thermonuclear weapons deployed at the height of the Cold War, the US Titan (ICBM) intercontinental ballistic missile (9 megatons) and the Soviet SS-18 ICBM (25 megatons), could each entirely destroy any of the world's largest cities in a single detonation.[2]

The United States and Soviet Union also developed large arsenals of chemical weapons, together accumulating in excess of 80,000 tonnes of active agent.[3]

In addition to the processes of weaponisation, the Cold War had three other effects. One was the mass diversion of monetary resources away from social welfare and developmental priorities, and a second was the diversion of intellectual and technical resources away from civil research and development into military programmes. Most significant, however, was the diversion of conflict from the direct superpower confrontation to 'proxy' wars fought indirectly between the superpowers.

Worldwide conflicts during the 1945 to 2000 period are thought to have caused 25 million deaths and 75 million serious injuries,[4] but many of these were fought under the shadow of the Cold War and included Korea, Vietnam, Afghanistan and the Horn of Africa. Such proxy wars caused around 10 million deaths and 30 million serious injuries.[5]

The idea that the Cold War was a period in which nuclear weapons kept the peace is a myth.

We also now know that the nuclear arms race was every bit as dangerous as the more radical anti-nuclear campaigners claimed at the time. As the archives are opened up and former opponents meet to compare their experiences, it is clear that crises such as Cuba (1962) and Able Archer (1983) were far more dangerous than was previously realised.[6] Moreover, there are known to have been a number of incidents in which nuclear weapons were lost and never recovered, and others in which nuclear weapons were damaged, came remarkably close to accidental detonation or where there was substantial radioactive contamination. The former included one US and two Soviet submarines in the 1960s and 1980s and the latter included accidents involving US B-52 strategic nuclear bombers in the 1960s.

One of the lessons from this brief excursion into Cold War history is that there is a persistent tendency by the authorities to maintain an aura of control and responsibility, when this is very far from what is actually happening. An impression of 'being in control' is a prerequisite for preventing the challenging of dangerous policies, but is frequently entirely false.

Forces in Transition

The early 1990s were marked by three major developments in military postures and deployments. The first was that the states of the former Soviet Union experienced massive economic problems leading, among other things, to the near collapse of their armed forces. Russia, in particular, lost most of its armed forces and was hard-pressed to engage in the internal war in Chechnya, let alone maintain an internationally significant force.

Secondly, a combination of multilateral and unilateral nuclear disarmament measures resulted in nuclear arsenals in Russia and the United States decreasing from around 70,000 to 20,000, although supplies of core fissile material in the withdrawn weapons were not irreversibly deactivated. There was also a significant international agreement to ban chemical weapons, the Chemical Weapons Convention, and this has resulted in the destruction of the large chemical arsenals – a technically difficult process that will take some years to complete.

Finally, the United States embarked on a progressive transformation of its armed forces. There were substantial decreases in Cold War-type deployments such as heavy armour in Europe and the anti-submarine warfare systems of the US Navy, but this was accompanied by the maintenance and even enhancement of forces intended to fight more limited wars at a distance. Amphibious forces, aircraft carriers, long-range air strike capabilities and Special Forces were all emphasised in the 'global reach' outlook, as well as more concentration on national and theatre missile defence.

By the end of the 1990s the United States was the only country with a true global reach, with just the UK and France having limited capabilities, and the tendency to use military force to maintain an 'aura of control' was firmly entrenched.[7]

The 9/11 Attacks and After

Prior to 9/11, the Bush administration had come to power with a very strong strand of neoconservatism embedded in its foreign and security policy. Multilateral approaches to arms control were seen as constraining and inappropriate: the Comprehensive Test Ban Treaty and the Anti-Ballistic Missile Treaty were not considered useful to the United States, there was opposition to the new International Criminal Court and withdrawal from the Kyoto accords. Of perhaps greater significance, if largely unrecognised at the time, was the refusal of the Bush administration to support the strengthening of the 1972 Biological and Toxin Weapons Convention.

Behind all this lay a belief in the New American Century: that the United States had a mission to encourage a world political and economic system that followed the American model. As one commentator remarked, the United States was not just any hegemon, it ran a uniquely benign imperium.[8] The world would be a safer place if it followed the American ideal.

The 9/11 attacks were a particularly grievous assault on this concept and the response was immediate. The Taliban regime in Afghanistan was rapidly terminated, an 'axis of evil' comprising Iran, Iraq and North Korea was identified and a policy of early pre-emption of potential threats was enunciated as part of a wider 'Bush doctrine'. Within eighteen months of 9/11, a second regime, that of Saddam Hussein, was ready for termination. In the past five years, as discussed earlier, wars have been fought in Afghanistan and Iraq that have together resulted in the deaths of well over 50,000 civilians and serious injury to many tens of thousands more, and up to 20,000 people are detained without trial in Iraq, Afghanistan, Guantánamo and elsewhere. This has resulted in a massive US military presence in the region.

Even so, Islamic terrorist groups inspired by the al-Qaida ideology remain highly active, more so than in the five years before 9/11, and numerous attacks have been staged in the Middle East, South and South East Asia and Western Europe. The United States has around 145,000 troops in Iraq engaged in a bitter and increasingly chaotic insurgency that is currently degenerating into a civil war, and a further 20,000 troops in Afghanistan fighting a counter-insurgency campaign. No end is in sight for either conflict and, as already discussed, there is every reason to see the Persian Gulf region, in particular, as a focus for long-term conflict.

Weapons of Mass Destruction

Meanwhile, the largely unstructured progress on nuclear arms control and disarmament of the early 1990s has been replaced by a surge in modernisation and proliferation, and there appears to be no possibility whatsoever of progress on the control of biological weapons. The biological issue has considerable potential significance and is one that governments should address with urgency.

The 1972 Biological and Toxin Weapons Convention (BTWC) is a worldwide convention banning such weapons, but it does not have any verification of inspection procedures built into it. Without teeth it is primarily a 'paper' treaty. This

● *US military base*

The majority of US bases are extensive autonomous bases.
Others consist of a significant US presence stationed at a host country's facilities.

The US has many smaller facilities in Iraq, Pakistan, Oman, Bahrain, UAE, Qatar, Tajikistan and Afghanistan.

Map of the Middle East showing US military bases in the region.

is in contrast to the more recent Chemical Weapons Convention (1997), which does have such procedures. Given the capacity for biological weapons to be produced using fairly widespread technical competences, this is a substantial problem that remains unresolved.

In practice, biological weapons were not regarded as

hugely significant systems for modern warfare, primarily because most agents, apart from anthrax and some others, did not have the necessary characteristics to make them effective. What is changing is that major developments in genetic manipulation and biotechnology give rise to the prospect of the development of effective biological agents.[9]

This was recognised nearly a decade ago and sustained efforts to strengthen the treaty started in Geneva shortly afterwards. After more than six years of negotiations, the process was effectively abandoned some three years ago. The attitudes of several countries proved problematic but it was the Bush administration that caused the most substantial difficulties, being strongly opposed to its domestic biotechnology industries being open to international inspection.

As of now, prospects for re-engaging in the process of getting an effective treaty are very limited yet, without an effective treaty, there is a real risk that biological warfare systems will become, for the first time ever, highly effective.

On the nuclear side, Britain, France and China are all engaged in processes to modernise their nuclear systems. In the case of the UK and France, their modernised systems are more flexible, have a longer range and are more accurate than older systems, and both countries have policies of first use, not just against nuclear-armed opponents but against the use or even the potential use of chemical and biological weapons.

Russia is trying to reconstitute an effective strategic arsenal and is beginning to modernise some strategic systems and, in the context of weak conventional forces, is more committed to nuclear first-use. Israel maintains a substantial nuclear force, and India and Pakistan are both vigorously developing their smaller forces, with Pakistan now planning to build a reactor enabling it to use the more efficient plutonium route to nuclear weapons.

North Korea started testing in October 2006, causing considerable international unease, and now probably has a very small stock of nuclear weapons. Iran is developing a civil nuclear power programme that would at least give it the potential to break out into nuclear weapons status.

The United States has already modernised one nuclear system, the B61-11 earth-penetrating warhead and is researching the Robust Nuclear Earth Penetrator, a system with much greater potential for use against deeply buried targets such as command centres or nuclear or biological weapon development facilities.[10]

More generally, the US nuclear posture is evolving into an outlook that envisages the pre-emptive use of nuclear weapons against states that may be seeking to acquire their own nuclear arsenals, but it goes further than this. What is clear is that the United States is moving towards a nuclear posture that envisages a range of small, lower yield, precise and more 'usable' nuclear weapons that are particularly suited for operations against deeply buried targets. This includes the maintenance of such weapons on a high alert status in a posture that envisages pre-emptive strikes.

The overall impact of nuclear weapon modernisations in states with nuclear weapons is likely to serve as a substantial encouragement to nuclear proliferation, as countries such as Iran, with their perceptions of vulnerability, deem it necessary to develop their own deterrent capabilities.

In broad historical terms, the first fifty years of the nuclear age, 1945 to 1995, saw the proliferation of nuclear weapons to just six countries (United States, USSR/Russia, UK, France, China and Israel), even if the United States and USSR deployed nuclear weapons in many countries. During this era, Brazil and Argentina withdrew from a mutual potential nuclear arms race in the 1980s, South Africa gave up its small arsenal in the early 1990s, and three post-Soviet countries (Belarus, Ukraine and Kazakhstan) returned Cold War-era nuclear arsenals to Russia. In the sixth decade of the nuclear age, 1995 to 2005, India has weaponised its nuclear capabilities, Pakistan has gone nuclear, North Korea probably now has a small cluster of nuclear warheads and there is a possibility that Iran may follow suit.

We are now at a potential 'tipping point' for nuclear proliferation. In East Asia, now that North Korea has carried out nuclear tests, there is a risk that countries such as Japan, South Korea and Taiwan will look again at whether they should develop nuclear weapons. In the Middle East, Iran has been declared by President Bush to be part of the 'axis of evil' and has seen the United States terminate regimes in two neighbouring countries. It is at least likely to develop the technical capabilities to produce nuclear weapons, even if it does not develop a nuclear arsenal. Even so, that may be enough to make other countries in the region, including Egypt, Turkey and Saudi Arabia, look at whether they should develop nuclear weapons programmes.

Nuclear Weapons Free Zones – an Untold Success Story

In September 2006, five former republics of the Soviet Union in Central Asia created the world's newest nuclear-free zone. The governments of Kazakhstan, Kyrgyzstan, Tajikistan, Turkmenistan and Uzbekistan signed the treaty, which bans the production, acquisition or deployment of nuclear weapons or their components as well as nuclear explosives, and forbids the hosting or transport of nuclear weapons or materials for third parties. The agreement is an important step forward for the global non-proliferation regime at a time when that order is under assault on multiple fronts.

It is not widely known that almost the entire Southern Hemisphere is already covered by Nuclear Weapons Free Zones (NWFZ), established by successive binding treaties since the 1960s. Three entire continents – South America, Africa, and Australasia – are NWFZs, along with the South Pacific and South East Asia.

Two key initiatives have recently been launched ~

In this environment, the 2005 Review Conference of the Treaty on the Non-Proliferation of Nuclear Weapons (NPT) in New York achieved nothing of note, and there are no prospects of bringing into force an effective Comprehensive Test Ban Treaty. The current situation is quite different from that at the height of the Cold War. In that era there was a small but clear risk of an all-out central nuclear exchange that would have which aim to extend this principle further. The first is a NWFZ for the Middle East. This proposal was most recently considered at a meeting of the International Atomic Energy Agency in September 2006, when fifteen Middle East countries (including Iran, Iraq, Syria, Jordan, and Egypt) called on Israel to join the nuclear Non-Proliferation Treaty.

The second initiative is a European one. Sixteen years after the end of the cold war, US nuclear weapons remain in Europe under NATO nuclear sharing arrangements, spread across Germany, Belgium, Italy, the Netherlands, Turkey and the UK. A motion has recently been put to the European Parliament calling for the withdrawal of US nuclear weapons from European territory by the end of 2006. This follows an overwhelming vote for this course of action in the Belgian Parliament.

These initiatives may flounder if there is not massive public pressure on politicians and diplomats. Everyone can support individuals and organisations pushing for these vital steps.

been an utter global catastrophe, what has been described as 'into the abyss'. The situation is now more akin to a 'slippery slope' in which there is an increasing risk of smaller scale use of nuclear weapons. This might be in circumstances that do not lead on to global nuclear war but have the dangerous effect of breaking the sixty-year nuclear threshold, taking us into an era in which nuclear weapons are seen as available weapons of war, with all the attending consequences.

These dangerous trends will be exacerbated by developments in directed energy weapons (lasers) and a race towards the weaponisation of space, as the United States remains determined to maintain its dominance there.

This determination is hard to overestimate. A new space directive signed by President Bush in 2006 states that 'freedom of action in space is as important to the United States as air power and sea power.[11] The directive went largely unnoticed at the time, but it is essentially a claim that America can do what it likes in space, and it rejects any new treaties or arms control agreements that attempt to limit US activities there, stating that the US will also deny adversaries the use of space capabilities hostile to national interests. Fears are that the United States is now laying the groundwork for a dangerous weaponisation of space.

This is a worrying trend, particularly when combined with the administration's commitment to a national missile defence system and its interest in promoting regional missile defence in East Asia, even if this incites an escalatory Chinese reaction. States such as China and Russia will not accept a situation in which the United States will have the unique combination of offensive nuclear forces and defensive systems, nor will they accept a US dominance of space, as this would represent a near-revolution in warfare and geopolitics.

An enhanced and renewed nuclear arms race is one likely outcome, combined with the competitive and uncontrolled weaponisation of space – a situation that must be avoided.

Area Impact Weapons

While most attention is focused on trying to control weapons of mass destruction, it remains the case that developments in conventional weapons put increasing numbers of people at risk.

There is frequent talk of precision-guided weapons, so-called 'weapons against real estate' that are so accurate that they can destroy targets without killing bystanders. Leaving aside the frequent presence of civilians in apparent military targets, and the frequent mistakes that are made in targeting, this ignores the parallel development of area impact weapons. These are devices such as cluster bombs, multiple rocket launchers and thermobaric (fuel-air explosive) weapons that are specifically designed to kill and maim people over the widest area possible.

A single BL755 cluster bomb, produced in the UK by Huntings and exported to many countries, disperses 147 grenade-sized 'bomblets', each of which explodes to produce 2,000 high-velocity shrapnel fragments. Each bomb disperses the bomblets over an area of more than two acres and has a devastating effect against what are euphemistically called 'soft targets', such as human beings.

Many industrialised countries now produce and export similar weapons and these have the potential to cause massive civilian casualties. Moreover it is common for a significant minority of the bomblets to fail to explode when dispersed, acting like anti-personnel landmines for months or years afterwards. In the 2006 war in Lebanon, Israel dispersed a million cluster bomblets, with tens of thousands remaining ready to explode long after the conflict had ended.

While some progress has been made in limiting the production of anti-personnel land mines, cluster munitions, thermobaric weapons and other area impact munitions are not currently subject to any arms control agreements. This is a situation that must be changed.

Overview

- The current focus is on maintaining international security by the vigorous use of military force combined with the development of both nuclear and conventional weapons systems; the first five years of the 'war on terror' suggest that this is failing.
- A brief history of the Cold War shows that there is a persistent tendency by the authorities to maintain an aura of control and responsibility, when this is very far from what is actually happening.
- Post-Cold War nuclear developments involve the modernisation and proliferation of nuclear systems, with an increasing risk of limited nuclear weapons use in warfare – breaking a threshold that has held for sixty years.
- Biological weapons have the potential to become effective weapons of war, given likely developments in genetic manipulation and biotechnology. The negotiation of a much-strengthened Biological and Toxin Weapons Convention should be a priority.

6.

The Way Forward

I just want you to know that, when we talk about war, we're really talking about peace.

George W. Bush

War is Peace. Freedom is Slavery. Ignorance is strength.

George Orwell, *1984*

We have undertaken a wide-ranging assessment of the variety of threats to global security. Among these international terrorism is only one, and in terms of lives lost, a relatively minor one. The response to terrorism needs to be placed in a broader perspective, to take account of economic, health, environmental and other long-term threats to human survival and well-being. Current responses to terrorism may, at best, ignore these broader trends, or at worst, actually contribute to them – making future terrorist attacks *more* likely, not less likely.

Our analysis concludes that future insecurity will actually arise out of four main groups of factors:

- the adverse effects of climate change and global warming
- competition for increasingly scarce resources, especially oil
- increasing socio-economic divisions and the marginalisation of the majority world
- the increased use of military force and the further spread of military technologies (including WMD)

However, an increasingly ineffective 'war on terror' continues to dominate government policies. The security agenda is being hijacked by this 'war' and the related conflicts in the Middle East. This, together with the continued pursuit of narrow national and economic interests, is distracting political elites from the genuine threats that humanity faces, causing their responses to these threats to be inappropriate and wholly inadequate.

Future Priorities

Of these threats, climate change is one of the most important problems facing the world community, and the effects of climate change on international security and human well-being will be profound. In particular, it now seems probable that climate change will have a massive effect on the world's tropical regions, primarily by decreasing rainfall over the land masses and thereby reducing the carrying-capacity of most of the world's existing major croplands, resulting in persistent food shortages and even famines that would lead to increased human suffering, greater social unrest, revised patterns of living and greatly increased migration.

For this reason alone, a fundamental transition from fossil fuels to renewables, along with a more rigorous approach to energy conservation, must be a core long-term aim. One of the key fossil fuel resources – oil – is also already a focus for major conflict and it is almost certain that, on present trends, instability and conflict will persist in the Persian Gulf region.

In essence, there are therefore two distinct reasons why rapid movement away from reliance on fossil fuels in general, and oil in particular, should be at the core of future energy policies. While climate change is widely recognised as one of these, conflict in the Persian Gulf over oil security is far less readily acknowledged. Climate change is becoming steadily more recognised by non-activists as a key issue, but its actual impact is still in its early stages of development. Oil insecurity, on the other hand, is already here, and is evidenced by the ongoing conflict in the Gulf. If the two are put together, it is much easier to advocate a move to renewable, low-carbon and carbon-neutral energy sources (including hydrogen fuel cells and biofuels for transport) as essential for short-term as well as longer-term reasons.

While climate change will undoubtedly overshadow every other issue of international security in the coming decades, it is the deepening global socio-economic divisions that will almost certainly be one of the most serious trends. It is in this context that the marginalised majority is more likely to support political violence against the rich minorities of the world. While middle-power states may be unwilling to accept the dominance of the West, Western leaders will nonetheless try to maintain the status quo and safeguard their access to resources, particularly Persian Gulf oil, by military means if necessary. It is safe to assume that socio-economic divisions will worsen, exacerbated by the effects of climate change, and taking place in a world where military technologies will proliferate.

Ensuring the control of both nuclear and biological weapons should therefore be considered as a core aspect of government policy, even though neither is currently prominent in the public eye. Opportunities to control nuclear weapons were lost in the late 1940s, the mid-1960s and the early 1990s, and this might be the best remaining opportunity to avoid the evolution of a world system involving further proliferation of nuclear weapons and a tendency to see them as usable in limited wars. The biological weapon problem is still one for the future, but trends in genetic manipulation make this a matter for urgent action now.

In terms of conventional military systems, one of the main effects of the 9/11 attacks and the pre-existing neoconservative attitudes in the United States has been to see military responses as the prime methods for maintaining international control. However, the experience of the first five years of the 'war on terror' indicates the need for a substantial rethink of this stance. It is now essential to develop alternative security strategies, and to devote greater effort and resources to promoting them.

In relation to international terrorism, in addition to the trends already discussed, a factor largely ignored by the US administration is the effects of cutting military aid budgets to African nations that have refused to sign agreements exempting American troops from the jurisdiction of the International Criminal Court in the Hague. While military aid is understandably controversial, Pentagon officials and senior military commanders are arguing that cutting these budgets undermines efforts to combat the rising threat of al-Qaida and other Islamist movements in several African countries, particularly Kenya and Mali. These aid cuts have also given China the upper hand as it spends millions of dollars on infrastructure projects and military training in Africa to help cement contracts for natural resources in the continent, especially oil.[1]

If America continues to pursue an unproductive and expensive 'war on terror' it may face an erosion of its economic and moral power that will make it unable to counter this strengthened China. As China continues to rise, and more countries realise that the US may not be able to guarantee their security, more governments may turn to China, and other powerful but undemocratic states, for both security and trade.[2] Another such country is Iran which, although the focus of much US attention over its nuclear programme, has greatly increased its influence across the Middle East and Asia in recent years – particularly in Afghanistan, Iraq and southern Lebanon – in large part thanks to the failure in the region of the 'war on terror'.[3]

The point here is not whether a rising China, or Iran, is a positive or negative development, it is that the US is implementing policies in one area that are offsetting progress in another. By not having an integrated approach to security, many of its policies are ultimately doomed to failure – and this, of course, is not a failing unique to the United States.

Overshadowing all of this will be the increasing problem of overpopulation, particularly in the developing world. By 2050, the populations of Chad, Mali, Guinea Bissau, Liberia, Niger, Burundi and Malawi are projected to triple in size, with Uganda growing even faster.[4] Efforts to combat poverty in some of the world's poorest countries will fail unless urgent action is taken to reverse this trend. With increased competition for scarce resources conflict is likely to increase, with the consequences felt well beyond Africa as migration causes further strains, particularly in Europe.[5]

Related to this are future regional concerns including the near-term effects of HIV/AIDS in Africa and the longer-term impacts of climate change on the tropical regions. Instability in the Persian Gulf and the wider Middle East is likely to grow as a result of conflict, particularly conflict related to securing oil supplies, and there is likely to be competition between the United States and China over those supplies. There is also a further risk of conflict between the United States and China over the issue of Taiwan's independence. While the serious crisis over Iran's alleged nuclear weapons programme looks likely to deepen and could potentially result in US or Israeli air strikes, future progress on the Israeli–Palestinian peace process, as well as further diplomatic links between Israel and Muslim countries, may eventually bring some stability to the region.

Many European countries, but especially the UK and other US allies, will face an increased level of threat from home-grown radical elements in response, in large part, to Western foreign policy in relation to the Middle East. This will give rise to calls for a change in policy. Russia and some of the Eastern European countries may also face increased levels of Islamist terrorism, but mostly as a result of harsh internal counter-terrorism measures and military action against jihadi militants (many with separatist agendas) either within or close to their national borders.

Finally, many Central and South American countries, especially the oil-exporting countries such as Ecuador, will undoubtedly experience violent and coordinated social unrest as a result of widening socio-economic divisions and the marginalisation of the poor, particularly the rural, shanty-town and indigenous populations. This could be even worse if, as in previous years, the United States once again focuses some of its attention on the region, and feels the need to intervene owing to left-wing and anti-American governments being elected there.

On the positive side, the ongoing reduction in inter-state conflict that has been occurring since the end of the Cold War, particularly between established democracies, looks likely to continue – although this may be offset by further military interventions by the United States and its allies.

In the short term, security strategies that demand further social control may just about keep the growing instability and violence elsewhere at bay, but this will only serve to intensify such instability in the long term. However, the continuing problems with insurgencies in Iraq and Afghanistan, as well as the failure to control the activities of the al-Qaida movement and Israel's failure to defeat Hezbollah in Lebanon, may well make it obvious that a sustainable alternative to the current US-led security paradigm of a 'war on terror' and pre-emptive military strikes is long overdue.

Sustainable Security

9/11 was an extreme event and presented a serious shock to the international system and American perceptions of invulnerability. In situations of shock, the key impulse of any leadership is to take the initiative to regain the appearance of control as soon as possible. It is remarkable how quickly and effectively the US government was able to project international terrorism as the greatest security threat facing the world, and gain adherents for this view, not only among American citizens, but in capitals and boardrooms around the world. 9/11 allowed the Bush administration to elevate some of the most divisive and counter-productive elements of the pre-9/11 security strategy, including unilateralism, pre-emptive military strikes against potential (not necessarily actual) threats, and aggressive counter-proliferation.[6]

So complete has the dominance of this US-led agenda

become that in just over five years it has become current security orthodoxy, an approach that might be called the 'control paradigm'.

This control paradigm puts forward the following responses to the threats we have discussed:

1) **Competition over resources.** An obsession with national energy security through taking control of, or gaining access to, key resources such as Persian Gulf oil, which leads to further conflict and tension in the region. This is the single most dangerous element of the current approach.

2) **Climate change.** An unshakable and unrealistic belief in the capacity of technological advances (including new generation civil nuclear reactors) operating within free markets as the primary means of responding to what some still consider the 'myth' of climate change.

3) **Marginalisation of the majority world.** Problems of poverty and socio-economic divisions are largely ignored as a security issue. But when immediate threats to the 'homeland' are perceived, the usual response is heavy societal control in an attempt 'keep the lid on' civil discontent, which only makes matters worse in the long term. Coupled with this is a belief that the free market will enable people to work their way out of poverty.

4) **International terrorism.** A series of counter-productive, controversial and often illegal counter-terrorism measures and attacks on civil liberties, including indefinite detention of terrorist suspects without trial and the 'extraordinary rendition' of suspects to countries that are known to use torture.

5) **Global militarisation.** Counter-proliferation measures focused on preventing WMD materials being acquired by terrorist groups or 'rogue states' considered to sponsor terrorism. Where it is believed that actors already possess, or are close to acquiring WMDs, a strategy of pre-emptive military strikes has been initiated.

This approach of attempting to maintain the status quo through military means and 'keeping the lid on' insecurity without addressing the root causes will not work in the long term and, in fact, is already failing in the face of increased paramilitary action and asymmetric warfare.[7] The current approach to security is deeply flawed, and is distracting the world's political elites from developing realistic and sustainable solutions to the non-traditional threats facing the world, among which terrorism is by no means the greatest or most serious.

Furthermore, people today often believe that the world is more violent and feel powerless to end the conflict.[8] This is despite the fact that the evidence shows that in the past decade armed conflict has declined dramatically in almost every region, and those conflicts that do occur are proving to be

The Failure of Current Strategies

When judged by its own goals it becomes clear that the 'control paradigm' is failing:

- Support for political Islam is increasing worldwide.
- The number of significant terrorist attacks is on the rise.
- Peace and democracy are elusive in the Middle East.
- The price of oil remains volatile and increases with every new crisis.
- The rich–poor divide continues to widen.
- Iraq is in a state of bloody chaos nearing civil war.
- The Taliban is a re-emerging force in Afghanistan.
- Iran, Syria and North Korea are increasingly emboldened.
- US strategic influence is waning, especially in Africa and the Middle East.
- Hezbollah have been able to claim a propaganda victory over Israel in Lebanon.
- The United States is increasingly viewed as the greatest threat to world peace.

less deadly.[9] While much of the blame for this inaccurate perception must lie with the media and the nature of its reporting of conflict and terrorism, some blame must also fall to those charged with keeping us safe: not only are the policies they are pursuing failing in many regards, they also do not make us *feel* safe.

Throughout this book we have outlined numerous general recommendations that would make a real difference and improve the chances for security over the coming decades. Of these recommendations, the key elements of a sustainable response might be:

1) **Competition over resources.** Comprehensive energy efficiency, recycling and resource conservation and management policies and practices. This would be coupled with large-scale funding for alternatives to oil.

2) **Climate change.** Introduction of a carbon tax and rapid replacement of carbon-based energy sources by diversified local renewable sources as the primary basis of future energy generation.

3) **Marginalisation of the majority world.** Reform of global systems of trade, aid and debt relief in order to make poverty reduction a world priority.

4) **International terrorism.** Addressing the legitimate political grievances and aspirations of marginalised groups, coupled with intelligence-led counter-terrorism police operations against violent revolutionary groups and dialogue with terrorist leaderships wherever possible.

5) **Global militarisation.** Alongside non-proliferation measures, states with nuclear weapons must take bold, visible and substantial steps towards disarmament, at the same time as halting initiatives such as the development of new nuclear weapons and new bio-weapons.

Together these constitute elements of a new approach, which we call 'sustainable security'. The main difference between this and current strategies is that this approach does not attempt to control threats unilaterally through the use of force ('attack the symptoms'), but rather it aims to resolve cooperatively the root causes of those threats using the most effective means available ('cure the disease'). In this way, a sustainable approach is inherently preventative, in that it addresses the likely causes of conflict and instability well before the ill-effects are felt, rather than waiting until the crisis is under way and then attempting to control the situation, at which point it is often too late.

Given that individual governments have repeatedly demonstrated their inability to deal with these problems effectively, it follows that this cooperative approach must be coordinated through a reformed United Nations, as individual governments or 'coalitions' are too focused on their own interests and tend to compartmentalise threats. Without an integrated strategy, progress in one area will be offset by failures in another.

This analysis can be summarised, albeit simplistically, in a diagram representing a five-rung 'ladder' of the key causes of instability, each of which negatively impacts on the other rungs.

Contrary to the claims of some, this approach to security does not underestimate the impact of the terrorist threat. Terrorism – as with any deliberate targeting of civilians – is a disgraceful and terrible tactic that is deeply traumatic for those affected by it. It should never be glorified or excused; but it *must* be understood. It is not enough to simply say it is 'evil' and therefore close down all further discussion. What we have tried to do is explore some of the root causes of international terrorism and to put terrorism in perspective in comparison with other threats.

Governments have finite resources, and must deploy those resources in ways that best ensure our security. A truly effective strategy would tackle and police immediate dangers whilst implementing policy changes to address longer-term trends that fuel terrorist recruitment, finance, legitimacy and effectiveness. The current approach prioritises the former; a sustainable approach would commit as many if not more resources to the latter.[10]

This is not 'soft on terrorism'; it is not appeasement. It is an attempt to understand the root causes of terrorism in order to better separate terrorist groups from their wider support base and reduce the motivations that lead to violence.

In the same manner, our analysis is not a 'left-wing' attack on US foreign policy. Neither is it an idealist's perspective: we are proposing realistic and integrated responses to realistic threats. Many of our conclusions, though of course not all, are shared by official sources such as the United Nations,[11]

The 'ladder of instability' (right).

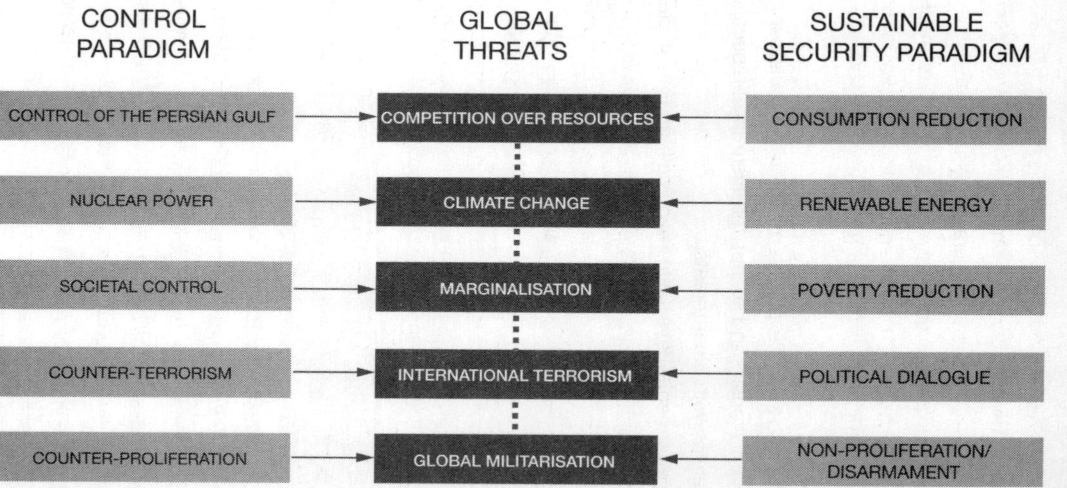
CONTROL PARADIGM
GLOBAL THREATS
SUSTAINABLE SECURITY PARADIGM
CONTROL OF THE PERSIAN GULF
COMPETITION OVER RESOURCES
CONSUMPTION REDUCTION
NUCLEAR POWER
CLIMATE CHANGE
RENEWABLE ENERGY
SOCIETAL CONTROL
MARGINALISATION
POVERTY REDUCTION
COUNTER-TERRORISM
INTERNATIONAL TERRORISM
POLITICAL DIALOGUE
COUNTER-PROLIFERATION
GLOBAL MILITARISATION
NON-PROLIFERATION/ DISARMAMENT

Sustainable Approaches to Terrorism

A sustainable security approach to terrorism would include:

- Rapid coalition troop withdrawals from Iraq, replaced by a UN stabilisation force, with US recognition that a client state or puppet regime cannot be sought there.
- The closure of Guantánamo Bay, the cessation of 'extraordinary renditions', and the observance of the Geneva Convention on detainees.
- Sustained aid for the reconstruction and development of Iraq and Afghanistan.
- A genuine commitment to a viable two-state solution to the Israeli–Palestinian conflict, and third-party brokerage of the wider Arab–Israeli confrontation.
- A firm and public commitment to a diplomatic solution to the current crisis with Iran.
- Police targeting of the international funding networks that support terrorism.
- An opening of political dialogue with terrorist leaderships wherever possible.
- Intelligence-led counter-terrorism police operations against violent revolutionary groups.

the UK Ministry of Defence[12] and even US intelligence agencies.[13] This is important as it shows that many areas of government and especially the military are already recognising the limits of current narrow definitions of security and the failure of solely military responses to threats to that security.

Perhaps two of the most striking examples of this come, surprisingly, from America. The first was a June 2006 survey by the influential American journal *Foreign Policy* which found that a large majority of America's leading foreign policy experts – including former senior members of the US government, military and intelligence agencies – believe that the US is losing the 'war on terror', that the government needs to think more creatively about the real threats to the world, and that the single most important thing that America can do to win the so-called 'war on terror' is reduce its dependence on foreign oil.[14]

The second was a September 2006 report from the Princeton Project on National Security. Over two years, the Princeton University project team consulted with more than 400 US foreign policy experts from both sides of the political divide – including prominent neoconservatives. They concluded that a new strategy designed to address multiple threats was needed, and criticised the Bush administration for framing the struggle against terrorism as a war similar to the Second World War or the Cold War.[15]

Over the next decade, a radical shift towards sustainable approaches to security will be hugely important. If there is no change in thinking, Western security policy will continue to be based on the mistaken assumption that the status quo can be maintained: an elite minority can maintain its position, environmental problems can be marginalised, and the lid can be kept on dissent and insecurity. In this scenario, little attempt will be made to address the core causes of insecurity, even if failure to do so threatens the elite minority as well as the marginalised majority.

Alternatively, a change in thinking could lead to an era of substantial progress in developing a more socially just and environmentally sustainable world order.[16]

Making a Difference

We recognise that the issues discussed in this book may seem too large for a single individual to do anything about. In one regard this is true – so many of these issues require action from above, from governments and transnational bodies such as the UN. However, they also require action from below, from ordinary people around the world. As Anita Roddick, founder of The Body Shop, has said: if you think you are too small to have an impact, try going to bed with a mosquito in the room.

At the personal level, anyone can make a difference because we can all *consume less, and do more*.

So many of the problems facing us are directly linked to our unrestrained consumption of the earth's finite resources. Each of us can therefore make a difference by following the maxim 'reduce, reuse, recycle'. This means consuming less by reusing, repairing and recycling that which we already have, and working out simple ways of reducing and altering the energy and other resources that we use in our daily lives. We can all make simple but effective lifestyle changes that can limit our impact on this planet.

We must then maximise our individual actions by doing more – supporting charities, lobbying representatives, buying locally and ethically, campaigning for change – the individual actions will differ depending on the opportunities and dangers in each country, but the effects are the same. We can all be active citizens; and we can all offer our support to others trying to do the same thing.

Through this combination of consuming less and doing more, the individual can genuinely make a difference, which when extended to the national or international level is when change can really begin to happen. There is a list of selected resources at the end of this book (plus extensive notes and references) that can help you to learn more about the issues we have been discussing and explore ideas for action and groups to join. There are millions of people around the world who are trying to make a difference through promoting sustainable ideas and actions. Connecting to others is a powerful antidote to the hopelessness that it is easy to feel in the face of such enormous problems.

However, what is ultimately needed is recognition by *governments* that current security measures will be ineffective in the long term and that a radical re-think of what is meant by 'security' is long overdue.

The sustainable approaches to future threats which we have outlined, need developing into fully workable security policies – and they need to be implemented. As already mentioned, though, this is unlikely to happen without pressure and support from below because these issues are sometimes seen as distant concerns by politicians – who are reluctant to dedicate resources now for benefits in the far off future – whereas terrorism, for example, is much more immediate and alarmist.

Therefore, the question for those of us concerned with promoting peace and security must now be: how are governments going to move beyond the current situation in order to promote sustainable global security for all?

None of the facts we have presented in this book are new. But they keep slipping out of current thinking and down the political agenda. What is needed right now, to put world leaders back on track, is the power and influence of ordinary people, who care that the world will be a fit place for their grandchildren to live.

NGOs, charities, schools, businesses, religious groups, journalists and citizens will need to work together to educate, promote action, raise awareness and convince the government that this new sustainable approach is practical and effective, and is the only real way to ensure security because it is realistic about the nature and extent of the threats to humanity and how we should respond to those threats. New leadership in the United States and UK in the coming years may well present the ideal opportunity for progress on this front. Genuine reform of regional organisations and the United Nations, particularly the Security Council, may also help governments move beyond the current narrow national and economic interests that are barriers to global stability. Furthermore, the energy and resources currently devoted to opposing war (anti-war) could be harnessed into positive efforts to promote peace and security (pro-peace). This is because an anti-war stance focused on a specific conflict does not address the structural changes needed to avoid future wars.

We need an integrated approach. For example, it is no longer enough to focus on environmental issues in isolation from the threat of socio-economic divisions and marginalisation discussed in this book. What we have argued is that all these issues are interconnected, and that governments must address environmental issues with reference to those of development and security (and vice versa). Working on one of these issues in isolation from the other two no longer makes sense; measures are needed which simultaneously ensure environmental protection, sustainable development and global security. This calls for a new approach, linking the peace movement with the anti-poverty and environmental movements.

The issues discussed in this book are those that are likely to dominate the international security environment over the next thirty years. Unless urgent action is taken in the next five to ten years, it will be extremely difficult, if not impossible, to avoid a highly unstable global system by the middle years of the century. Governments, NGOs and concerned citizens must work together and recognise that we now all have an urgent responsibility to embrace a sustainable approach to our planet's future.

This book is a wake-up call – we hope it has inspired you to new action. The solutions to the problems we face already exist, and it is not too late to change the dangerous course we are on. There is no better time to act than now.

Resources for Change

Whatever you can do, or dream you can do, begin it. Boldness has genius, power, and magic in it.

W.H. Murray

Global citizen empowerment and action has been transformed by the Internet. With Internet access and a search engine such as Google, almost unlimited resources are at your fingertips. Many of the resources we provide below can be most conveniently accessed through the web. If you can afford to buy this book, and have access to places where it is sold, then you are almost bound to have access to the Internet, if not at home, then in your workplace, public library, school, college, or Internet café.

However, most of the world's population do not have access to the Internet, and this is one telling indicator of the dire state of global wealth inequalities. Even in many of these countries though, public libraries, local newspapers and local radio stations will provide extensive information and resources for residents, including details of local activities and groups.

Resources are listed here under the four main threat categories covered in this book: (1) climate change, (2) competition over resources, (3) marginalisation of the majority world, and (4) global militarisation. This is followed by a section of general resources related to sustainable security and other issues covered by this book. They are further subdivided into *Learn* (resources focused on accessible information and analysis) and *Act* (resources focused on things that you can do).

Because we are English-speaking authors based in the UK, this list contains mainly English-language materials, and some materials that focus on UK issues. For that we apologise. We have also tried to focus on resources from people and organisations that share our integrated approach to threats and sustainable responses to those threats.

1) Climate Change

Learn

The New Economics Foundation

www.neweconomics.org

The Foundation has an environmental programme that looks at the impact of climate change on global poverty reduction and the impact of rich country lifestyles. Its central call is that 'lifestyles must become sustainable'.

An Inconvenient Truth: The Planetary Emergency of Global Warming and What We Can Do About It

Al Gore (Bloomsbury, 2006)

The former US vice president issues a wake-up call to America and the world on global warming and the fact that we are going to have to change the way we live our lives. Also now a major motion picture from Paramount, available on DVD.

Act

The Green Alliance

www.green-alliance.org.uk

The Green Alliance is a membership organisation that works to promote sustainable development by ensuring that the environment is at the heart of decision-making.

Climate Care

www.climatecare.org

When you fly, drive, and heat your home, your CO_2 emissions add to climate change. Climate Care lets you offset these emissions by funding sustainable energy projects. Also see www.carbonfootprint.com.

Greenpeace International

www.greenpeace.org/~climate

Greenpeace is asking you to take part in an energy revolution: to go from a world powered by nuclear and fossil fuels to one running on renewable energy. Their website includes a section on taking action which includes steps you can take to save energy.

Stop Climate Chaos

www.stopclimatechaos.org

Works to build a massive coalition that will create an irresistible public mandate for political action to stop human-induced climate change. Nothing on this scale has been attempted before on climate change and this is your chance to get involved.

2) Competition over Resources

Learn

Half Gone: Oil, Gas, Hot Air and the Global Energy Crisis

Jeremy Leggett (Portobello Books, 2005)

This book exposes the true status of the world's energy

supplies, revealing both the scale of the disaster and the action everyone must take to stand a chance of averting it.

Blood and Oil: The Dangers and Consequences of America's Growing Dependency on Imported Petroleum
Michael Klare (Metropolitan Books, 2004)
The world's rapidly growing economy is dependent on oil, the supply is running out and the United States is engaged in an escalating game of brinkmanship to secure its continued free flow. Michael Klare argues that the solution to America's foreign-oil dilemma is not diversification away from the Middle East, but to reduce consumption by sharply rising fuel prices.

The Energy Saving Trust
www.est.org.uk
The trust provides independent evidence-based policy analysis around the areas of energy efficiency, small-scale renewable technologies such as solar PV, small-scale wind and ground source heat pumps and clean, low carbon transport, covering both the UK and Europe.

Act

Green Solutions
www.green-solutions.com
This site is packed full of useful information and links which should help you to make more sustainable lifestyle decisions. That means minimising your impact on your surrounding environment, which includes your social and economic environment.

Reduce, Reuse, Recycle

www.reducereuserecycle.co.uk

An online green guide that provides information on environmental issues, recycling and saving the earth's precious resources.

WaterAid

www.wateraid.org

WaterAid is an international charity dedicated to helping people escape the stranglehold of poverty and disease caused by living without safe water. They aim to help 1 million people gain access to water by 2010, but to do so they need your support.

3) Marginalisation of the Majority World

Learn

The Millennium Development Goals

http://www.un.org/millenniumgoals

Find out more about progress towards the UN's Millennium Development Goals agreed by world leaders in 2000. These range from halving extreme poverty to halting the spread of HIV/AIDS and providing universal primary education, all by the target date of 2015.

Making Terrorism History

Scilla Elworthy and Gabrielle Rifkind (Rider, 2006)

This book shows why political violence is now such a major force in our world and explores some of the issues surrounding the links between marginalisation and fundamentalism. At the same time it gives a range of practical actions that can be taken to combat terrorism, not only by our governments but also on the ground in Iraq, Israel, Palestine and in our local communities.

Act

Jubilee Debt Campaign

www.jubileedebtcampaign.org

Join the campaign to demand an end to the scandal of poor countries paying money to the rich world and call for 100 per cent cancellation of unpayable and unfair poor country debts.

Make Poverty History

www.makepovertyhistory.org

The biggest ever anti-poverty movement came together under the banner of Make Poverty History in 2005. The fight against poverty continues. Take action now to pressure politicians and decision-makers to help make poverty history. Also see www.maketradefair.com.

Amnesty International

http://www.amnesty.org/actnow

Amnesty International is a worldwide movement of people who campaign for internationally recognised human rights. Their website includes many ways you can get involved and support their important work around the world.

Ethical Consumer

www.ethicalconsumer.org

Promotes universal human rights and environmental

sustainability by providing information on consumer issues which empowers individuals and organisations to act ethically in the market place.

4) Global Militarisation

Learn

War Prevention Works: 50 Stories of People Resolving Conflict
Dylan Matthews (Oxford Research Group, 2001)
Fifty short accounts from all over the world of what ordinary people are doing to stop war and conflict – armed only with integrity, stamina and courage.

Human Security Report 2005: War and Peace in the 21st Century
Human Security Centre (Oxford University Press, 2005)
www.humansecurityreport.info
This report documents a dramatic, but largely unknown, decline in the number of wars, genocides and human rights' abuses over the past decade. The report argues that the single most compelling explanation for these changes is found in the unprecedented upsurge of international activism, spearheaded by the UN, which took place in the wake of the Cold War.

The WMD Awareness Programme
www.comeclean.org.uk
The blurring of the distinction between chemical/biological/nuclear, and even other types of weapons, by using the overall term WMD, clouds the issue. The WMD

Awareness Programme was created to remove this confusion about WMD by bringing honesty, transparency and accountability into this field. They make reliable information available to all through their website.

International Alert

www.international-alert.org

International Alert is an independent peace-building organisation working in over twenty countries and territories around the world. It works directly with people affected by violent conflict as well as at government, EU and UN levels to shape both policy and practice in building sustainable peace.

Act

Peace Direct

www.peacedirect.org

Peace Direct supports grassroots peace-building in conflict areas. In every conflict, there are local people working for peace. Peace Direct funds their work, promotes it and learns from it. With Peace Direct, you can support practical action to build a more peaceful world.

Abolition 2000

www.abolition2000.org

This campaign is a network of over 2,000 groups around the world working for the abolition of nuclear weapons by 2020. Their website includes lots of links to activities in the UK and across Europe.

5) Other Resources

Learn

Losing Control: Global Security in the Twenty-First Century
Paul Rogers (Pluto Press, 2002)
This book argues that the current Western security posture is one of elite societies maintaining their power in an increasingly divided and environmentally constrained world. It concludes that a new approach to global security is necessary in which the reversal of socio-economic polarisation and the enhancement of sustainable development are placed at the heart of Western security policies in the early twenty-first century.

Al-Qaeda: The True Story of Radical Islam
Jason Burke (Penguin Books, 2004)
The author provides a wide-ranging and coherent description of the rise of radical Islam, and a persuasive analysis of how the conditions which the world is now facing have come into being. In doing so, he explodes a number of the myths and illustrates how the failure of governments around the world to act on the conditions which foster radicalism has contributed more to its rise than the actions of any individual or group.

***sustainable*security.org**
www.sustainablesecurity.org
This website provides the latest news, analysis and research relating to threats to global security and sustainable responses to those threats, with a focus on the UK, United States and

Middle East. You can also subscribe to a weekly e-bulletin of all the latest articles and news from the site.

Worldwatch Institute

www.worldwatch.org

The Worldwatch Institute offers a blend of interdisciplinary research, global focus, and accessible writing that has made it a leading source of information on the interactions among key environmental, social, and economic trends. Their work revolves around the transition to an environmentally sustainable and socially just society – and how to achieve it.

Act

365 Ways to Change the World

Michael Norton (Myriad Editions, 2006) www.365act.org

Packed with ideas and facts from leading campaigning organisations, this handbook suggests one action for every day of the year. All can be planned or carried out by individuals from home or their computer.

Oxford Research Group

www.oxfordresearchgroup.org.uk

Oxford Research Group (ORG) uses a combination of innovative publications, expert roundtables, residential consultations, and engagement with opinion-formers and government, to develop and promote sustainable global security strategies. It publishes monthly international security briefings which you can subscribe to and has a supporter programme. All royalties from sales of this book will go towards ORG's work.

Notes and References

1. A Clear and Present Danger?

1. Jean-Marie Colombani, 'Nous sommes tous Américains', *Le Monde* (12 September 2001).
2. Committee on the Present Danger www.fightingterror.org
3. Jim Lobe, 'They're Back: Neocons Revive the Committee on the Present Danger, This Time Against Terrorism', *Foreign Policy in Focus* (21 July 2004).
4. See, Secretary-General's High-Level Panel on Threats, Challenges and Change, *A More Secure World: Our Shared Responsibility* (New York: United Nations, 2004).
5. 'Poverty warning after US attacks', *BBC News* (1 October 2001).
6. Gregory Foster and Louise Wise, 'Sustainable Security: Transnational Environmental Threats and Foreign Policy', *Harvard International Review*, Vol. 21, No. 4 (Fall 1999), pp.20–3.

2. Climate Change

1. Peter Schwartz and Doug Randall, *An Abrupt Climate Change Scenario and Its Implications for United States National Security* (Global Business Network, October 2003).
2. 'Storm Warning: The hurricane forecast is becoming clearer, and the news is not good', *New Scientist* (24 September 2005).
3. David King, 'Climate Change Science: Adapt, Mitigate or Ignore?', *Science*, 303 (5655), pp.176–7 (2004).
4. John Ashton, 'World's most wanted: climate change', *BBC News* (8 September 2006).
5. Intergovernmental Panel on Climate Change, *Climate Change 2001: The Scientific Basis* (United Nations, 2001).
6. David King, *The Science of Climate Change: Adapt, Mitigate or Ignore?* (Ninth Zuckerman Lecture, 2002).
7. Intergovernmental Panel on Climate Change, op cit.
8. Norman Myers, 'Environmental Refugees in a Globally Warmed World', *Bioscience*, Vol. 43, No. 11 (December 1993), pp.752–61.
9. Jonathan Patz, Diarmid Campbell-Lendrum, Tracey Holloway and Jonathan Foley, 'Impact of Regional Climate Change on Human Health', *Nature* (17 November 2005).
10. Emma Duncan, 'The heat is on: A survey of climate change', *Economist* (9 September 2006).
11. Steve Connor, 'Global Warming past point of no return', *Independent* (16 September 2005).
12. David Rind, 'Drying Out the Tropics', *New Scientist* (6 May 1995).
13. John Vidal and Tim Radford, 'One in Six Countries Facing Food Shortage', *Guardian* (30 June 2005).

14. Michael McCarthy, 'The century of drought', *Independent* (4 October 2006).

15. Intergovernmental Panel on Climate Change, op cit.

16. US National Oceanic & Atmospheric Administration (NOAA), *After Two Large Annual Gains, Rate of Atmospheric CO_2 Increase Returns to Average* (31 March 2005) http://www.noaanews.noaa.gov/stories2005/s2412.htm

17. Steve Connor, 'US Climate Policy Bigger Threat to World than Terrorism', *Independent* (9 January 2004).

18. Michael McCarthy, 'China Crisis: threat to the global environment', *Independent* (19 October 2005).

19. Gerard Wynn, 'Exxon misleads on climate change – UK Royal Society', Reuters (21 September 2006).

20. ExxonMobil, 'Public Information and Policy Research', *2005 Corporate Citizenship Report*, http://www.exxonmobil.com/Corporate/Files/Corporate/giving05_policy.pdf

21. Center for the Study of Carbon Dioxide and Global Change, http://www.co2science.org/scripts/CO2ScienceB2C/about/position/globalwarming.jsp.

22. George Monbiot, 'The denial industry', *Guardian* (19 September 2006).

23. Paul Rogers, *The Risk of Nuclear Terrorism in Britain* (Oxford: Oxford Research Group, 2006).

24. Frank Barnaby and Shaun Burnie, *Thinking the Unthinkable: Japanese Nuclear Power and Proliferation in East Asia* (Oxford: Oxford Research Group, 2005).

25. Royal Commission on Environmental Pollution, *Sixth Report: Nuclear Power and the Environment* (London: Her Majesty's Stationery Office, 1976).

26. Jan-Willem Storm van Leeuwen and Philip Smith, *Nuclear Power: the Energy Balance* (August 2005) www.storm-smith.nl
27. Sustainable Development Commission, *The Role of Nuclear Power in a Low Carbon Economy* (London: SDC, 2006).
28. Environmental Audit Committee, *Keeping the Lights On: Nuclear, Renewables and Climate Change,* Volume 1 (London: Stationery Office, 2006).
29. Harry Lehmann, *Energy Rich Japan* (Aachen: Institute for Sustainable Solutions and Innovations, 2003).
30. Environmental Change Institute, Submission to the Science and Technology Select Committee of the House of Lords: 'The Practicalities of Developing Renewable Energy Stand-by Capacity and Intermittency' (University of Oxford, 2004).
31. Graham Sinden, *Wind Power and the UK Wind Resource* (Oxford: Environmental Change Institute, University of Oxford, 2005).
32. Frank Barnaby, Keith Barnham and Malcolm Savidge, Memorandum to the Environmental Audit Committee Inquiry 'Keeping the Lights on: Nuclear, Renewables and Climate Change' (Oxford Research Group, September 2005).
33. Chris Langley, *Soldiers in the Laboratory: Military Involvement in Science and Technology and Some Alternatives* (Folkestone: Scientists for Global Responsibility, 2005).
34. Stockholm International Peace Research Institute, *Recent Trends in Military Expenditure* http://www.sipri.org/contents/milap/milex/mex_trends.html.

3. Competition Over Resources

1. Donella H. Meadows, Jorgen Randers and Dennis L. Meadows, *Limits to Growth* (London: Earth Island, 1972).
2. Belinda Coote, *The Trade Trap: Poverty and the Global Commodity Markets* (Oxford: Oxfam Publishing, 1992).
3. China became a net importer of oil more recently, in 1993, but import demands are now rising rapidly.
4. Paul Rogers and Malcolm Dando, *A Violent Peace* (London: Brassey's, 1992).
5. *BP Statistical Review of World Energy 2005* (June 2005) http://www.bp.com/genericsection.do?categoryId=92&contentId=7005893
6. The firing of Kuwaiti oil wells by retreating Iraqi forces in 1991 was only feasible because of this.
7. A 'caliph' is the term or title for the Islamic leader of the *Ummah*, or community of Islam. A 'caliphate' is the office or territorial jurisdiction of a caliph.
8. Paul Rogers, *Iraq and the War on Terror: Twelve Months of Insurgency 2004/2005* (London: I.B. Tauris, 2005).
9. Joint Doctrine and Concepts Centre, *Strategic Trends: Methodology, Key Findings and Shocks* (Ministry of Defence, 2003).
10. Intergovernmental Panel on Climate Change, op cit.
11. 'Study Highlights Global Decline', *BBC News* (30 March 2005) http://news.bbc.co.uk/1/hi/sci/tech/4391835.stm
12. Jessica Williams, *50 Facts That Should Change the World* (Cambridge: Icon Books, 2004).

4. Marginalisation of the Majority World

1. US Department of State, *Patterns of Global Terrorism* (reports from 1995–2003) http://www.state.gov/s/ct/rls/crt
2. A total number of 2,689 US citizens were killed in international terrorist attacks in 2001. See, US Department of State, *Patterns of Global Terrorism 2003 – Statistical Review* http://www.state.gov/s/ct/rls/crt/2003/33777.htm
3. Center for Disease Control, *National Vital Statistics Reports*, Vol. 52, No. 3 (18 September 2003).
4. The Henry J. Kaiser Family Foundation, *US Federal Funding for HIV/AIDS: The FY 2006 Budget Request* (HIV/AIDS Policy Fact Sheet, February 2005) http://www.kff.org/hivaids/upload/Fact-Sheet-U-S-Federal-Funding-for-HIV-AIDS-The-FY-2006-Budget-Request.pdf
5. Steven Kosiak, *Overview of the Administration's FY 2006 Request for Homeland Security* (Center for Strategic and Budgetary Assessments, May 2005) http://www.csbaonline.org/4Publications/Archive/U.20050503.FY06HomelandSecBudget/U.20050503.FY06HomelandSecBudget.pdf
6. World Health Organisation, *World Health Report 2004* http://www.who.int/whr/2004/en
7. Rory Carroll and Sarah Boseley, 'The Greatest Catastrophe: Aids worst disaster in history, says UN chief', *Guardian* (10 December 2004).
8. UNAIDS, *Financing the Expanded Response to AIDS* (July 2004) www.unaids.org/bangkok2004/docs/Financing2response.pdf
9. See, http://www.unicef.org/uniteforchildren/index.html
10. Human Security Centre, *Human Security Report 2005: War*

and Peace in the 21st Century (New York: Oxford University Press, 2005), p.137.

11. Andrew Koch, 'Briefing: The US in Africa', *Jane's Defence Weekly* (12 January 2005).

12. 'Security Council resolution 1308 (2000) on the responsibility of the Security Council in the maintenance of international peace and security: HIV/AIDS and international peacekeeping operations', *United Nations* (17 July 2000).

13. Human Security Centre, op cit.

14. United Nations Development Programme, *United Nations Human Development Report 2005* http://hdr.undp.org/reports/global/2005

15. Rory Carroll and Sarah Boseley, op. cit.

16. Save the Children, *Rewriting the Future: Education for Children in Conflict-Affected Countries* (September 2006).

17. United Nations Development Programme, op. cit.

18. The United Nations World Food Programme reports that one in nearly seven people do not get enough food to be healthy and lead an active life, making hunger and malnutrition the number one risk to health worldwide – greater than AIDS, malaria and tuberculosis combined. See http://www.wfp.org

19. International Action Network on Small Arms, www.iansa.org

20. Amy Belasco, *The Cost of Iraq, Afghanistan and Enhanced Base Security Since 9/11* (CRS Report for Congress, October 2005) http://www.fas.org/sgp/crs/natsec/RL33110.pdf

21. In July 2005, Iraq Body Count and Oxford Research Group reported that 24,864 Iraqi civilians had been reported killed and at least 42,500 wounded between 20 March 2003 and 19 March 2005, with US-led forces alone being responsible

for 37 per cent of the deaths. See, Iraq Body Count, *A Dossier of Civilian Casualties in Iraq, 2003–2005* (Oxford: Oxford Research Group, 2005). By 28 September 2006, Iraq Body Count were reporting that between 43,525 and 48,317 civilians had been reported killed in Iraq. See www.iraqbodycount.org

22. On 28 September 2006, Iraq Coalition Casualty Count were reporting 2,709 US military fatalities since January 2003. In addition, 20,468 US military personnel had been wounded in action. See http://icasualties.org/oif

23. 'Iraq: The Uncounted', *CBS News* (21 November 2004) http://www.cbsnews.com/stories/2004/11/19/60minutes/main656756.shtml; Scott Shane, 'A Flood of Troubled Soldiers is in the Offing, Experts Predict', *New York Times* (16 December 2004).

24. Iraq Coalition Casualty Count, op cit.

25. Professor Marc Herold of the University of New Hampshire estimated that a minimum of 3,100–3,500 Afghan civilians were killed as a direct result of US bombing between October 2001 and February 2002 (this does not include persons dying later from injuries, hunger, disease or cold). See, Marc W. Herold, 'US Bombing and Afghan Civilian Deaths: Official Neglect of "Unworthy" Bodies', *International Journal of Urban and Regional Research*, Vol. 26, No. 3 (September 2003). Official figures put the number of people killed in the 9/11 terrorist attacks at around 2,900. See, *The 9/11 Commission Report* http://www.9-11commission.gov/report/911Report.pdf and Center for Disease Control, 'Deaths in the World Trade Center Terrorist Attacks – New York City, 2001', *Morbidity and Mortality Weekly Report*, Vol. 51 (11 September 2002).

26. Pew Global Attitudes Project, *America's Image Slips, but Allies Share US Concerns over Iran, Hamas* (Pew Research Center, June 2006).

27. See, Paul Rogers, *Iran: Consequences of a War* (Oxford: Oxford Research Group, 2006).

28. David Beetham, *The War in Iraq and the Future of Democracy, East and West*, paper presented at the Centre for Democratisation Studies, University of Leeds (12 February 2003).

29. Kishore Mahbubani, 'The impending demise of the postwar system', *Survival*, Vol. 47, No. 4 (December 2005).

30. Sanjay Suri, 'War Provoking Terror, Amnesty Says', *Inter Press Service* (23 May 2006).

31. Defense Science Board, *Report of the Defense Science Board Task Force on Strategic Communication* (Department of Defense, September 2004) p.48.

32. 'Tackling Extremism and Radicalisation: Working Group Report', in *Preventing Extremism Together* (Home Office, October 2005), p.90.

33. 'Poll reveals terror target fears', *Guardian* (21 August 2006).

34. According to CNN/USA Today/Gallup polls from November 2001 to January 2006. See, http://www.pollingreport.com/terror2.htm

35. According to CBS News polls from October 2001 to January 2006. See, http://www.pollingreport.com/terror2.htm

36. Jason Burke, *Al-Qaeda: The True Story of Radical Islam* (London: Penguin Books, 2004).

37. Paul Rogers, 'Al-Qaida: a question of leadership', *Open Democracy* (17 November 2005).

38. Pew Global Attitudes Project, *The Great Divide: How Westerners and Muslims View Each Other* (Pew Research Center, June 2006).

39. Jason Burke, op. cit., p.39.

40. National Intelligence Estimate, *Trends in Global Terrorism: Implications for the United States* (National Intelligence Board, April 2006). Declassified key judgements posted at http://www.globalsecurity.org/intell/library/reports/2006/nie_global-terror-trends_apr2006.htm

41. Robert Pape, *Dying to Win: The Strategic Logic of Suicide Terrorism* (Random House, 2005).

42. Scilla Elworthy and Gabrielle Rifkind, *Hearts and Minds: Human Security Approaches to Political Violence* (London: Demos, 2005).

43. Prince El Hassan bin Talal, 'Rebuilding lives is the key to lasting peace', *Jane's Defence Weekly* (9 November 2005).

5. Global Militarisation

1. See successive editions of: Ruth Leger Sivard, *World Military and Social Expenditure* (Washington DC: World Priorities Inc).

2. Paul Rogers, *A Guide to Nuclear Weapons* (Oxford: Berg Publishers, 1988).

3. For details of chemical arsenals during and after the Cold War, see successive editions of: *SIPRI Yearbook: Armaments, Disarmament and International Security* (Stockholm: Stockholm International Peace Research Institute).

4. See, Ruth Leger Sivard, op. cit.

5. Paul Rogers, 'A World Becoming More Peaceful?', *Open Democracy* (17 October 2005).

6. Able Archer was a test of NATO's nuclear-release procedures, but the Soviet leadership thought that the war games were a cover for an imminent NATO attack and

placed nuclear-capable planes on standby at East German bases. Unlike the Cuban missile crisis, Able Archer happened without most of the world realising and it was not until afterwards that we learned how close we had come to nuclear war.

7. While the UK and France do have some global military projection, it is simply not on the same scale as the United States. For example, a single US aircraft carrier battle group has a more powerful military capability than all the aircraft carriers of Britain and France combined.

8. Charles Krauthammer, 'The Bush Doctrine: ABM, Kyoto and the New American Unilateralism', *The Weekly Standard* (4 June 2001).

9. See, the University of Bradford's project on *Preventing Biological Warfare: Strengthening the Biological and Toxin Weapons Convention*, http://www.brad.ac.uk/acad/sbtwc

10. Although the US Congress has withdrawn funding for this project, there are fears that it may continue under 'black programme' funding.

11. Office of Science and Technology Policy, http://www.ostp.gov/html/US%20National%20Space%20Policy.pdf

6. The Way Forward

1. Mark Mazzetti, 'US Cuts in Africa Aid Said to Hurt War on Terror', *New York Times* (23 July 2006).

2. Mark Katz, 'The global war on terror's long-term cost', *United Press International* (9 September 2006).

3. Chatham House, *Iran, its Neighbours and the Regional Crisis* (London: Chatham House, 2006).

4. Carl Haub, *2006 World Population Data Sheet* (Population

Reference Bureau, August 2006), pp. 5–6.

5. Xan Rice, 'Population Explosion Threatens to Trap Africa in Cycle of Poverty', *Guardian* (25 August 2006).
6. James Kemp, 'Sustainable Peace and Security in the 21st Century', *Compass* (forthcoming).
7. Paul Rogers, *Losing Control: Global Security in the Twenty-First Century* (London: Pluto Press, 2002).
8. 'Brits think violence rising', *Press Association* (21 September 2006).
9. Human Security Centre, op cit.
10. James Kemp, op cit.
11. See, for example, Secretary-General's High-Level Panel on Threats, Challenges and Change, op. cit.
12. See, for example, Joint Doctrine and Concepts Centre, op. cit.
13. See, for example, the National Intelligence Estimate, op cit.
14. Tom Regan, 'US must win war of ideas', *Christian Science Monitor* (16 June 2006).
15. Princeton Project on National Security, *Forging a World of Liberty Under Law: US National Security in the 21st Century* (Princeton: The Woodrow Wilson School of Public and International Affairs, 2006).
16. Paul Rogers, op cit.

Website addresses correct at time of publication.

Glossary

Al-Qaida A radical Islamist movement or international 'network of networks' which shares a commitment to using violence to achieve its broad political aims.

Axis of evil Term used by President Bush in his State of the Union Address on 29 January 2002 to describe 'regimes that sponsor terror'. Originally referring to Iraq, Iran and North Korea, and then later also Syria.

Global security An approach to international security which treats the world as a systemic whole, rather than focusing on the interactions of individual nation states, and promotes comprehensive, systematic and worldwide responses rooted in a deeper understanding of underlying trends and causes of insecurity and conflict.

Majority world Refers generally to the countries of Asia, Africa and Latin America. Used as an alternative term to describe the 'Third World', and reflects the fact that most of the world's population lives in developing countries.

Marginalisation The state of being considered unimportant, undesirable, unworthy, insignificant and different, resulting in inequity, unfairness, deprivation and lack of access to mainstream power.

Paradigm shift A significant change in human understanding from one predominant worldview (paradigm) to another previously thought impossible or unacceptable.

Rogue state A state which, according to the person using the term, operates outside the norms of the international community and, for example, attempts to acquire weapons of mass destruction, commits crimes against humanity, harbours terrorists, or seeks to overthrow or corrupt the political processes of other countries.

Sustainable security A sustainable approach to global security emphasising the long-term resolution of the root causes of insecurity and conflict.

War on terror An ongoing military and political campaign by the governments of the United States and its principal allies ostensibly aimed at destroying groups deemed to be 'terrorist' (primarily radical Islamist organisations such as al-Qaida) and ensuring that 'rogue states' no longer support terrorist activities.

Also available from Rider Books:

Making Terrorism History

Scilla Elworthy & Gabrielle Rifkind

Ever since 9/11 it's been clear that we need a new approach to terrorism. Clear, radical and extremely persuasive, *Making Terrorism History* explains the root causes of terrorism, the links between trauma and fundamentalism, as well as why peace processes sometimes collapse.

This important book also gives a range of practical actions that can be taken to combat terrorism, not only by our governments but on the ground in Iraq, Israel and Palestine, and more widely. In addition there are many simple but effective steps that we too can take within our local communities to make peace – not war – on terror.

'Essential reading for anyone who wishes to understand terrorism today'

Terry Waite, CBE